GETTING
TO
WHERE
YOU
ARE

ALSO BY STEVEN HARRISON

Doing Nothing

Being One

The Question to Life's Answers

The Happy Child

GETTING

TO

WHERE

YOU

ARE

*The Life
of Meditation*

STEVEN HARRISON

SENTIENT PUBLICATIONS, LLC

First Sentient Publications edition 2003
Copyright © 1999 by Steven Harrison

Printed in the United States of America

Cover design by Kim Johansen, Black Dog Design

Library of Congress Cataloging-in-Publication Data

Harrison, Steven, 1954-
    Getting to where you are : the life of meditation / Steven Harrison.—
1st Sentient Publications ed.
        p. cm.
    Originally published: New York : J.P. Tarcher/Putnam, c1999.
    ISBN 159181006X
        1. Meditation. I. Title.

BL627.H37 2003
291.4 35—dc21

                                                                2002042945

SENTIENT PUBLICATIONS
A Limited Liability Company
1113 Spruce Street
Boulder, CO 80302
www.sentientpublications.com

CONTENTS

PART THREE
WALKING-AROUND MEDITATION
AND EVERYDAY LIFE

GETTING TO WHERE YOU ARE

INTRODUCTION

One thing the world definitely does not need is another book on how to meditate. That is precisely why I have written a book on meditation. This book is written not as one more how-to book but to dispel the notion that there is some technique of meditation that will solve our problems, relax our bodies, and bring us to the radiant light of truth in twenty minutes a day.

There has been more harm done than help given in the propagation of spiritual teachings. The ideas of spirituality have become a burden in the lives of seekers, a pressure along with all the other pressures of life. This pressure is taken into our meditation, the very thing we take up to relieve ourselves.

Relax! We've got it wrong. Meditation is not about achieving some state of bliss, or even about relieving our anxieties. Meditation is not twenty minutes in the morning before a day of pressure. Meditation is about everything. We are already doing it, effortlessly. It is our natural state of existence.

This book is as much about what meditation is *not* as it is about what meditation is. In the end, meditation is about letting go of what isn't and being what is. How hard can it be to get to where you are?

Millions of Americans meditate. For most, meditation is a frustrating experience that is the result of authoritative teaching by self-created American instructors or imported exotic gurus and compounded by our misunderstanding of the way our minds actually operate.

Spirituality is replete with idealism and imagery, and because of this, meditation practitioners keep a secret. They have failed. They know what they are supposed to be experiencing. The secret is this: Nothing is happening during their meditations except the buzz of thought and the discomfort of the body.

In our consumer society, urban dwellers own four-wheel-drive sport utility vehicles, best-selling novels are bought not to be read but to decorate coffee tables, and brand-name merchandise is collected as a substitute for class. It should not be surprising, then, that the meditation du jour is ingested without result or understanding. For the marketers of meditation, content is less important than market share. New techniques are simply invented or old techniques repackaged to service the ever-fickle, consuming public.

After all, materialism doesn't work. Who is actually happy? Religion doesn't work. We pray, but who is listening? We try meditation, new therapies, exotic religions, angels, channels. Nothing works, nothing fundamentally resolves our conflict.

There has been a significant backwash from the psychospiritual movement of the last three decades because of the failure of these techniques. Millions of spiritually interested individuals religiously follow practices that have not fundamentally changed their lives—and never will. Equal millions have capitulated to their underlying cynicism as they discovered their teachers and peers mired in scandals involving sex, money, or power.

The dynamic exploration of psychology and spirituality of the past decades has given way to psychobabble, rote religious practice, and New Age jargon. Now what?

Getting to Where You Are was written to address this question by investigating the actualities of meditation without the overlay of a particular religion, belief, or technique. It is an invitation to the practitioner of any meditation technique to understand more about the actuality of meditation and of life. It is a deconstruction of the ideas that surround meditation and that obscure our understanding of it. This book describes meditation uncluttered by motivation, which is the simple recognition of where we are. This is the only meditation that does not produce more mind clutter than it removes, and it is the one that we are all doing already—actuality meditation—that is, living. This is the active exploration of the nature of life, free from the restraints of doctrine, religious belief, and technique-oriented practices.

Getting to Where You Are was written to free the reader from the burdens imposed by the dogmatic structures of meditation techniques and to replace it with . . . nothing—just the exuberance of a life investigated—a life well lived.

PART ONE

IS IT

TIME

TO

WAKE

UP?

HOW DID WE GET HERE?

*There is no cure for birth or death, save to enjoy
the interval.*

—George Santayana

BORN NAKED, COLD, AND HUNGRY —
THEN IT GETS WORSE

At some point in each of our lives, we suddenly become aware.
This could be when we are four or when we are forty. In a wild
moment of recognition, we look around at the world we inhabit
and there is the primal experience of—complete confusion.

We are flooded with more questions than we could possibly
handle in any lifetime. Who am I? Where did I come from?
Where am I going? What is death? Why is relationship so difficult and confusing?

The fact is, we really don't know who we are, how we got
here, what death is, let alone much about the relationships in our
lives. We are confused. We look for answers, anything that will
give us surety in the face of chaos. We turn to the myths of our
culture, the beliefs of our religion, the solace of a spiritual practice, or the authority of a charismatic leader. But none of these
things can end our confusion. We know that. And that fact is
even more confusing.

How is it that we appear in this world so unprepared to understand it? Why are we so full of questions and so devoid of

meaningful answers? We can try to avoid this existential state of uncertainty, but it is our constant companion. It is with us at any point when we question our beliefs. It is with us when the structures of our life undergo sudden change, or we fall ill, or a loved one dies. How did we get like this?

We were born in uncertainty. Where did the first breath come from? Will there be another? When will the last breath come? The very nature of our existence is tenuous, hanging moment by moment, breath by breath on some invisible, evanescent quality called Life.

The moment of birth is traumatic. We are born out of our mother's pain and into our own pain. We are born with nothing but that pain—naked, cold, and hungry. Then it gets worse.

We are poked, prodded, and weighed. Lights are turned on and off. Diapers. Blankets. People. We want to sleep. We want to eat. The world swirls around us and we enfold its swirling, not separate from it and yet not understanding it.

Through this all, we breathe. We are alive and vital. We are a bundle of genetic potential unfolding without explanation into a child, an adolescent, an adult, an aged human being just a moment from death, now taking our very last breath.

But we start naked. We start without knowing. We start in uncertainty.

We begin to learn. We cry and are fed. Or we cry and we are *not* fed. We cry and are held. Or we cry and we are slapped. Our experiences begin to form the basis for our reality, and those experiences are encoded in thought as memory. We learn relationships—our actions and the results, the interaction of our body and the objects around us, the means to find food, warmth, and sleep.

We crawl, we toddle, we walk. We are developing our skills, our knowledge, and our ability to influence those around us. Those around us provide us with food, warmth, and sleep. Influencing these providers becomes an important skill, and we are soon enveloped in a world of coercion, influence, and counterinfluence. We continue to learn and grow.

We have forgotten that we were born naked. We have even forgotten that we were born. From our perspective, we have always been here and, for that matter, we should always be here from now on. We just need to get that food, warmth, and sleep.

We have become enclosed in this world of forgetting. We grow up with this world of subject and object, force and counterforce, influence and counterinfluence as our context. Thought is our ally in the world because thought knows how to predict and mediate this new world. Soon thought is no longer our ally, thought is us. The useful tool that thought actually is, becomes our identity.

We have forgotten that there was any other way of being.

Our world becomes increasingly complex as our basic drives become extended into our new psychological world, a world centered on "me" and filled with "my" thoughts and feelings. In this world, body hunger becomes mind hunger. We need attention, we need recognition, we need affection, and the list goes on because the needs are endless. We apply what we learned about getting food to our psychological requirements. Our personality forms around our successes and failures. We learn *who* we are by *how* we do with the procurement of the responses we need.

We have forgotten that we have no idea where we came from.

We have forgotten the unindividuated world out of which our thoughts developed and coalesced around the core idea of self. We have put aside the uncertainty. We have formed a "me," a personality, a bundle of behaviors that function to get us what we need, or at the very least tell us who we are in each situation we encounter.

We are adults. We feel solid. We don't feel naked. We know what we like and what we don't like. We get confused sometimes. We get hurt sometimes. Well, we get hurt a lot, actually, but that's life, isn't it? Sure, it is. We'd love to talk more, but we have to go to work now and drop off the kids at school.

The kids? How did we get kids already? Weren't we just born, naked and all of that, just a moment ago? How did we get here? Where did we come from? Why do we die? And who *is* this person lying in bed next to me? The questions flood in again. The uncertainty. The confusion. Suddenly we are aware. We look around. We need some clues—and fast.

Jolted Awake in the Middle of a Life

We were just jolted awake in the middle of our life. We know vaguely how we got here. There are photo albums over on the bookshelf. There's some hard evidence there, some clues. There are our baby pictures. They look like a lot of babies, but you will recognize the nose. There are pictures of the toddler years, the first bicycle, the first day at school, the soccer team, the class play.

You can see the parents getting older, picture by picture,

changing into more of the same, just bigger and then fatter and then grayer. And then all of a sudden, the pictures start repeating themselves. Baby pictures that look like a lot of babies, but you will recognize the nose. Good God, those are our kids! Now they're toddlers. Now they're going to school. We're the ones getting fat and gray this time.

This could be serious. We're in the middle of our life and we haven't got a clue what is going on. And then, the first clue we find is that we are getting old. How did this happen?

I got the education because that's what you do. So, of course, I got an okay job, because I got the education. But that was only after a couple months bumming around Europe. I did the free-spirit thing. Then the house. That's what you do with the check from the job. You buy a house. Oh, right, almost forgot, the marriage. That came after the job, but before the house. Almost forgot the marriage because it's become like part of the furniture, if you know what I mean. It's not that we're not in love, it's just that we know each other so well there's not much to say. Anyway, then there were the kids. What a big deal that was. If you don't have kids, you'll never know what you're missing. But they're older now, getting ready to go off to get an education. I'm worried they won't get a good job. I'll probably have to help them get their first house. Now, what were we talking about?

The forgetting sets in. The mind reels on. The generations come and go.

One day, something shifts, we wake up and we can't forget. We can't go back to sleep. We have come face-to-face with a life that is so cluttered, so full of its obligations, its time and money pressures, its fears, yet so lacking in obvious meaning or any hope for a change.

Now what?

Life Clutter — I'll Simplify When I Get a Minute

Faced with the fundamental realization that we need to change the reality of our out-of-control lives, lives careening from task to task on the way to oblivion fueled only by our self-serving cynicism, we do the obvious—we procrastinate. We create time. I'll simplify when I get a minute. Later. Tomorrow. Next month. Next year. After the kids go to college. After I retire.

The problem with procrastination, of course, is that it doesn't work. Otherwise, it would be a truly beautiful quality of the human psyche.

Imagine, for a moment, that the garbage needs to be taken out. I'll do it tomorrow. I don't feel like it tonight. Procrastination at its finest. Effective. Precise. Problem solved, at least until tomorrow. Energy conserved. Tomorrow—same garbage, same problem, same response. I'll do it tomorrow. And so on, night after night. Month after month. Imagine, if this really worked.

In actuality, the garbage is piling up all over the house and rotting. Noxious gases are being released. Bugs have hatched out of the mess. The neighbors have called the health department.

Social Services has taken the kids. The mortgage company has decided to foreclose to protect its asset. Procrastination only works in our mind. It doesn't work in actuality.

This is obvious. Except when it comes to changing our lives. Change, we seem convinced, must always come later. Yet we really know that change must take place now. There is no other time or place for it to happen. There is only now. Our minds will tell us there is a later, but we know that later is piled high with rotting garbage, the uncleared clutter of our lives.

If we are to simplify, to declutter, to clear out our life, the time is now. The very realization of this fact brings us crashing through the labyrinth structures of procrastination into the present. The future has collapsed into this moment. We have discovered the key to change because we have discovered where change resides. We have discovered Now.

Now we have no more excuses. Now we have no more tomorrows. Now we have direct contact with the stuff of our life; we can feel the burden of the agreements and obligations that create the pressure of time, the endless drive into the future.

Now let's simplify. Now let's find the timeless quality of life that we know exists. Now let's find the very expression of our love and linkage with the world, the very meaning of our existence. Now let us engage the questions of life and death instead of avoiding them. Now let us relate honestly rather than strategically. Now let us connect rather than survive. Now let us face our fear rather than live out of that fear.

Now.

Who Are All These People in My Life?

We get it. We really get it this time. It's Now! It's not Later. Later is Never. This is it. We're ready for change. Out with the old, in with the new. First we'll clean out all the closets and send a carload over to the Salvation Army thrift shop. Then we'll get rid of all the stuff around the place, the stacks of books we'll never read, the television, the bed with the broken spring that our spouse is sleeping in. We'll even get rid of the spouse. Uh-oh, we forgot that we are in a relationship. We have agreements, a history, a future.

We have a problem. We're married to the problem. We gave birth to the problem. Or the problem parented us. Or befriended us. Or works with us. The problem is this: We have friends and family, co-workers and neighbors. They are integral to our life. To a large degree they define our life. We have a deal. Now we want to change. That isn't part of the deal.

Our friends and family like us just the way we are, even if they don't like us the way we are. They like not liking us the way we are. There is something very secure and comforting about knowing what to expect—like it or not—from somebody with whom you spend time. When we begin to change, we threaten this security. And this web of people, this web of influence, reacts in the only way it knows how.

It tries to hold back the change. It tries to coerce us to stay the same. It tries to terrorize us, make us feel guilty, ungrateful, self-centered, unreliable, or a host of other things, all of which are designed to keep us as we are.

Who are these people, anyway?

There are the parents. They gave birth to us, or at least raised us. This gives them the right to involve themselves in every detail of our life forever. This is a given. Or is it a taken? Who made up this rule, anyway? Isn't parenting a function that has a time and a place, but also has a time and a place to change into something else? Parents become so used to parenting that they often make a habit of it and continue parenting their children even after their children become adults. The result: middle-aged children and old parents, neither of whom can change.

Then there is the mate, husband, wife, boyfriend, girlfriend, or whatever. Here the plot thickens. Here we *did* participate in some agreements. We said we loved and in return we expected love. We created a social contract based on our deepest feelings. It is a key element of our life. But what are our deepest feelings? Where do they come from? Are they still our deepest feelings, or have we discovered even deeper feelings that are no longer re-flected in our contract? This part of our life needs change the most and it resists change the most.

Then the children. They didn't create themselves, we did. We created the relationship with them, the structures of agreement and disagreement. They are just living through it, trying very hard to get to adulthood where they can have a crack at making their own messy lives. These kids require everything from Band-Aids to braces, from saintly love to Solomonic wisdom. Plus you have to be able to spell obscure words, remember how to solve for x, and know what a ribosome is. This is the social contract from hell. We created the blank contract and signed it. We gave the blank contract to the kids, and they pretty much fill it in over our signatures.

The lesser players in our life are the co-workers and the boss, the neighbors and the friends. Here we share patterns and habits, location and work, recreation and diversion. These are predictable, measurable behaviors that establish relationships with others who also express these behaviors. The key here is that if you change your behavior, plan to change your friends. If you change your location, plan to change your neighbors. And if you change your attitude at work, plan to dust off your résumé and start seeking opportunities for professional advancement.

The people in our life expect certain things from us and we expect back. They are the very manifestation of the way we understand and relate to the world around us. We all know that there is something not quite right. There is a mechanical, repetitive quality to our lives and to our relationships. We have grown accustomed to this sleepwalking through our day and our years. But we know, down deep inside, that there has to be something more or different.

This dissatisfaction becomes more and more urgent. We find more and more need to change, to bring about more substance, more meaning, more depth to our life.

SELFISHNESS VS. SELFLESSNESS

The urgency for change can take us in the direction of selfishness or it can take us in the direction of selflessness. The movement toward selfishness is more likely. Our deep dissatisfaction can drive all our energy in the pursuit of whatever it takes to make us feel better. This is selfishness. This is the pursuit of money, fame, respect, sex, power—really anything that will fulfill our habitual desires.

We try on new identities. We do a makeover. We read self-help books. We take personal power seminars. We work out at the gym. We try to enhance our position in life—our power, our money, our position of control or dominance, or, at the least, our notoriety at home, at work, and in our community. If we run a corporation, we dominate the competitor. If we are the Girl Scout leader, our troop sells more cookies than anyone in the region.

The urgency that recognizes that we are stuck drives us to be something more. This "more" can also be more of a failure, more neurotic, more depressed. The search is for identity, so selfishness doesn't care if it takes us to success or to the perfect safety of failure.

Ironically this path to selfishness is a tremendously liberating direction for some of us. We actually fulfill the dicta of our selfish drives. We become powerful or we become failures. We consume ourselves in the self-centered life of our conditioning. And still the knowledge is there that we live only a mechanical and repetitive life. The emptiness is still there, despite the power, respect, money, and all the rest we may have created in our search for success. The drive for transcendence is still there, despite the world of neurotic entanglement, dependence, and depression we may have created in our search for failure. The urgency is still there.

In the achievements of selfishness, we may discover the limitations of selfishness.

Here the direction can seem to change. The movement toward selfishness now seems to recognize its own futility, and we begin to search for selflessness. We seek out the avenues to this magical state in the world around us. We try religion—new ones, old ones, reform ones, Eastern, Western, orthodox. We'll even try religions based on such outlandish concepts that you might think a science fiction writer made it all up. In fact, we might even try a religion that a science fiction writer *did* make up. In short, we'll suspend every bit of intelligence, feeling, intuition, and knowledge that we have in order to believe in the totally ridiculous—UFOs in comet tails coming to take us away; disembodied beings from other worlds chained to volcanoes millions of years ago; disincarnate ten-thousand-year-old warrior kings commenting on our problems.

We try desperately to believe. If we can just believe in something, anything, we know we will be fine. We try. We believe. We really believe. We make friends with other believers. We study our beliefs. We practice our beliefs.

In the end, we just can't do it.

We can't suspend everything for belief. The urgency is there. The unsettled quality that reminds us that we are living a mechanical, repetitive life is there.

We investigate spirituality, either to supplement our religious beliefs or to replace them. We try yoga, meditation, astrology. We are getting healthier, quieter, lighter. We talk the talk and we even walk some of the walk. We speak with authority about the heart chakra and our Moon in Capricorn. We sit in the lotus position, a rose crystal hanging from our necks, carefully chewing and tasting the freshness of the spinach and sprout salad with fat-free balsamic vinaigrette dressing. We have made great strides in this self-less-ness business. We are very enlightened.

Actually, we are very confused.

The urgency in our life has taken us to the facsimile of self-lessness. It looks like the real thing, but we know the fact. The self is in great shape, enjoying all the accoutrements of spirituality. From its narcissistic perspective, the "me" is better than ever.

The self has discovered selfishness in its pursuit of selflessness.

Now we are in a quandary. The movement to selfishness doesn't fulfill us. The movement to selflessness enmeshes us even deeper in our self.

The urgency remains. We flounder. We vacillate. Suddenly we stand absolutely still in the face of these contradictory movements. The urgency intensifies. We do not move. We have seen the endless cycles of getting somewhere and finding ourselves nowhere. For this one fresh moment, we give up trying, we give up getting anywhere different than where we are.

In the stillness of this moment, we have suddenly arrived, at long last, somewhere. We are here. In this moment. And in this moment, without a history and without a future, we are not selfish, nor have we found our way to selflessness. There simply is no one there. There is just the moment, the stillness.

And, just as suddenly, we are back. We have just had an amazing experience. We were free for a moment of the burden, the pain, the confusion of our life, because we were free of our self. Now we are back and we capture the experience in memory. We remember it. We begin to look for it. We must find that experience—the experience that is the absence of the experiencer.

We look. And we look. And we look.

We cannot find it again, because we are looking in all the wrong places. We are looking in the field of thought, of memory, of experience for that which is not-thought, which is not-memory, which is not-experience, which is not-me.

And so we begin searching for that which is only found when the searching ends. This search cannot find what it looks for. Its only hope is to exhaust itself and to come to the end of itself, the end of the spiritual search.

GETTING THROUGH WITH GETTING THROUGH

Life is just one damned thing after another.

—Elbert Hubbard

GETTING THROUGH THE DAY,
GETTING THROUGH THE BILLS,
GETTING THROUGH A CALL WITH MOM

A lot of what we do with our lives is simply to get through them. That's it. That's the accomplishment. We got through another day. We got the kids to school. We got to work. We got the oil changed in the car during the lunch hour. We got the presentation done. We got through rush-hour traffic. We got through the traffic of our lives. We survived.

This is quite an accomplishment, given the complexity and challenges of the contemporary world. But is it enough?

We are driven in our lives by forces we barely recognize. Each of us has an internal agenda that has been constructed from collected messages of assurance or critique and our underlying biological makeup. We are cautious or carefree, introverted or extroverted, detail or big-picture oriented, neat or messy. We have countless other attributes in combinations that follow our personally constructed reality and give us a sense of substance.

This individual construction is seamlessly joined to the social construction in which we fulfill the functions of parent, spouse, sibling, worker, entrepreneur, scientist, politician, soldier, or any number of other cogs in the wheel of societal life.

We know what to do each day based on our personal and social reality. These constructions give us order and security. They get us through the day.

If our motivation flags on a social level, we only need to look at the stack of bills piling up in order to find the energy to go to work. If our motivation flags on any level, we just need to answer the phone. It's a call from Mom.

Mothers appear to us as the translators of the whole of our personal and social reality. Sometimes it seems that they created reality. We know they created us, and that is a very daunting consideration. So when Mom says, "How is everything?" it's not just a simple greeting. The Creator is asking the Creation to substantiate the Creation's worth and significance. The Creator is indicating that the very act of creating the Creation could have been an error.

Getting through a call with Mom is one of the great challenges of life. If Mom buys our explanation of our life, then maybe we're on to something. Mostly Mom says, "Isn't that interesting . . ." and we know we haven't got it yet.

The fact is, we are in this together with Mom. She needs us to get it, to get through with getting through life, to demonstrate an intelligent life. Mom gave us her unfinished business to finish. She is watching in the hope that we will demonstrate a different possibility with our life. This possibility is the gift of the Mother.

She'll recognize it when she sees it. Anything less than that is . . . interesting.

If the message from life isn't clear, call your mother. You'll find out how you're doing pretty quickly. The message from Mom will be clear. Mothers are like that.

LESS IS MORE, MORE OR LESS

Man is the only creature that seems to have the time and energy to pump all his sewage out to sea, and then go swimming in it.

—Miles Kington

Less is more. This actually seems to be true, more or less. We pay a price for the complexity and clutter of our lives. We are owned by our possessions, controlled by our jobs, and we exist to fulfill our money obligations, and not simply to be fulfilled.

Simplify, simplify. Thoreau advised simplification, but that was before Walden Pond was ringed by housing developments.

What does it mean to simplify today? There is a growing simplification movement that counsels us on everything from grocery coupons to zero-coupon bonds. Simplification advisors suggest we translate our dollar purchases into the amount of time we spent earning the money and see if the trade-off is what we want. Nobody in his right mind would spend a year of life working in some dreary job in order to pay for a car to transport him to the dreary job. When we calculate how much we spend paying for the cost of working—income taxes, social security, transportation, insurance, food and day care—it starts to appear that it is not more profitable to work, but to work at *not* working and, more to the point, not spending.

Once we stop buying, we can start investing. We are supposed to spend a couple of decades living in a cheap basement apartment, eating beans we grew hydroponically in the bathtub, wearing clothes from the thrift store, riding a bicycle through the rain and snow instead of driving a car, and singing to ourselves to save on the cost of entertainment. We are advised to invest our savings in treasury bills. T-bills are favored by Japanese investors fleeing their crashing stock market, retired people in the last years of their life, and simplification advisers who did not make their personal fortunes investing in T-bills. In this theoretically Simple World, the resulting income will allow us to continue in the meager lifestyle we developed —without working. That is, unless inflation decreases the value of our T-Bills, in which case we can continue the spartan lifestyle—and work.

Perhaps for some, this Simple Life is appealing. For others it may appear to be a bit obsessive. Now instead of going to work to make the money to live, we stay home and work to not spend the money to live.

Isn't simplification something else altogether? Isn't the core of a simple life the recognition that we live in relationship whether we are working or not working? Isn't a simple life a balanced life, a life of inclusion and openness rather than anxiety and protectiveness?

For some of us, simplification will mean going to work, getting a more challenging job, starting a business, or increasing our marketable skills so that we can stabilize ourselves financially.

For some of us, simplification will be to recognize that we are overconsuming, driven by money, and working out of fear. For all of us, simplification can only come from understanding the interrelatedness of our life with the life around us.

Solving *our* problem doesn't solve *the* problem. Our problem is our money and our life. This problem can be solved by making a lot of money or by not spending a lot of money. It really doesn't matter which reality we construct to live in.

The real problem is the fact that our lives are lived in the isolation that fear brings with it. The real problem is that we are content to construct realities and to live within those boxes. The real problem is "me."

Real simplification, the only simplification, is not to deconstruct our work and money but to deconstruct our selves.

Stepping out of Our Screenplay . . . and Finding Ourselves in a New Screenplay

My only regret in the theater is that I could never sit out front and watch me.

—John Barrymore

We all like stories. We like to hear them and we like to tell them. Our favorite story is the one we have written, produced, and starred in. Whether it is a comedy, a drama, a tragedy, or an adventure, in our world this is the Really Greatest Story Ever Told, a blockbuster, all-time attendance-record-breaking, top-grossing phenomenon.

It is our story.

The Story of My Life.

Starring Me.

Screenplay by Me.

Adapted from the best-selling novel, *The Story of My Parents' Life*.

"Two thumbs up!"—Me

Admittedly the story is a bit formulaic. It has been told billions of times, in billions of ways. But we never tire of it.

In the beginning of the story we are born. This is a momentous event. After a childhood that is largely underscored by our sensitivities being crushed by parental disregard, we become adolescents. Here in riveting scenes we discover the depths of parental hypocrisy, the allure of our sexuality. Now we meet our downfall in drugs, alcohol, or other forms of confusion. Or maybe that happens later when we have our first failed marriage or failed business. Whatever.

The important thing is that it is mostly the fault of our parents, or our first husband, or our second wife, but we're in therapy trying to take responsibility for our life. That's hard to do with the life we've had. This is why we don't have enough money, love, health, or happiness. This is why we can't, we won't, or we shouldn't. This is why we are afraid. This is why we accept the stultifying oppression that our lives have become. This is why we are helpless victims of forces that we can't control. If only our parents had been better. But it is great just to be able to tell our story.

Okay, the story is a bit stale. It's been done before. But this story is different simply because it stars Me. That's what brings life into it. Me.

Or so we would like to believe. The fact is that the story is stale because the storyteller is stale.

We contain our life in a story that we have been telling for so long we've forgotten that we're telling it. We've overlooked that it is a retelling of our parents' story, our neighbors' story, our teachers' story. But we keep telling the story of our life, because we don't know what else to do.

We try to adapt the story, improve it, expand it, but it somehow always stays trite, shallow, and repetitive.

We tell the story because it serves to make some sense of the world around us. It gives us a reference point from which to act. It tells us how to act, and why. It tells us why we fail, why we are unhappy. Like all mythologies, it has gods and goddesses, demons and demonesses.

Without the story we wouldn't know where we have been or what to expect. Without the story, the storyteller, the writer, and producer, the "me" would become a has-been, useless, a real nobody.

We would become nothing.

No More Story Lines — The Final Curtain

The show is over when we realize it is a show. When we see clearly that the story is a story, that the storyteller is a story, that the "me" is a story, then the curtain falls. The applause is deafening only in its absolute silence.

We have discovered that at the core of our existence is not a center, but, like the proverbial onion, as we strip away each layer, in the end we come to nothing. Nothing is the center of our existence. There is no one at the core.

We may use the word *nothing* here, but it is not the word that is at our core. We could as easily say that at our center is everything. We could say it is love, or consciousness, or a vast field of awareness in which everything arises, including the very idea of our separate self.

What is at the core is not in language, it is not a subject or object, it is not in thought or word of any kind.

It is not divided, so it cannot be objectified.

It is not possessed, so it cannot be mine.

Here, at last, we find life itself.

Being without doing, a script gone silent, the greatest story ever untold.

IS THIS ALL THERE IS?

If you can keep your head when all about you are losing theirs, it's just possible that you haven't grasped the situation.

—Jean Kerr

A FUNDAMENTAL QUESTION

When we stop for a moment and survey the totality of our life—the relationships, the possessions, the successes and the failures, the hopes and dreams—we come face-to-face with a fundamental question: Is this all there is?

Is this all there is? Can this be it? This is what billions of years of physical organization of matter, several million years of organic organization, and thousands of years of social organization have led to? The electric bill due on the tenth of the month. A mocha latte at Starbucks. Slightly less sleep than we would like on a daily basis. Yoga class on Thursday night. A book on Tibetan Buddhism on the table by the bed. A sport utility vehicle that goes to work and back and picks up the kids at the soccer games. A primary relationship that is (a) imagined but nonexistent, (b) existent, new, possibly even exciting, but untested and untrusted, (c) existent, trusted, but a bit stale, or (d) none of the above.

Is this all there is? Are we really the expression, the culmination, of everything that has come before us? Is this really it?

Who Am I?

Out of the spiritual mythology of the last hundred years comes the story of a boy who came home from school in his small village in India one day and found himself contemplating the absurdity of his existence. Is this really it? How could it be? It couldn't be.

In his contemplation, he was overcome by an overpowering fear of his own death, the cessation of everything that he was and knew. Strangely enough, he did not run from this fear but decided to experience his death.

He lay down and, viewing his body from the mystic's perspective, he wondered, If the body dies, what remains? Who am I?

The boy, Ramana Maharshi, continued to contemplate the question "Who am I?" with such intensity that, as the lore is told, he found nothing that was permanently the self other than the vast silence of cosmic consciousness. He was canonized as a great saint, and an ashram was built around him. He lived the rest of his life teaching little more than the inquiry into the nature of the self until his death in the middle of this century.

What should we do with this story?

We can relate to its mythology (which is perhaps true and perhaps not). We can remember a great mystic who transcended the life that we live. We can inspire our own spiritual practices with his words and his picture. We can discuss what his life was and meant. We can find his disciples to learn from. Or the disciples of those disciples. We can even find fourth-generation disciples.

Or we can disregard all of the mythology, lineages, and teachings and ask the same question of ourselves. Who am I?

What is the nature of this central core sense of identity? Who is it that views reality? Who is it that lives and dies? What preexists this sense of self and what goes on after it ceases? Is the body the center of our universe? Is the body and its biomechanical processes who we are? Is this all there is?

These are not simply intellectual questions. These are existential questions, questions of our very being. These questions ask if the entirety can be known by us. Are we limited to the world that our thoughts describe? This small reality of thought . . . is this it?

The slightly mad monk sat down at the restaurant counter and
  ordered his meal.
"Did you see me come in?" he asked the waitress.
"Yes, I did," she replied.
"Have you ever seen me before?" the monk inquired.
"No, I haven't," said the waitress.
"Then how did you know it was me?"

LOOKING FOR CLUES

We will not find the answers to these questions in the mind, in the field of thought, simply because the field of thought does not include what is outside of thought—whatever that is. If we want to know the entirety, we must find what there is that can apprehend and give expression to the entirety.

If what we know is not "it," if there is "more," that "more" is not encompassed by the reality that thought can describe. We have found our first clue. We need more clues.

Where do we find these clues? We cannot find them in our ideas—these are within the field of thought. We cannot find them in our beliefs, or our parents' beliefs, or our cultural beliefs. We cannot find them in the teachings of the beliefs of others whether through a religion, a form of spirituality, or a teacher of spirituality. These are all still just social constructions in the conceptual world within which we seem to be stuck.

Our only clue so far is that "it" is not in the conceptual world. How do we discover what is *not* conceptual when the only tools we seem to have to work with are thought based?

Is our one clue enough with which to proceed? The only piece of the puzzle is this: Thought is only a part of the whole, and the whole cannot be contained in a part. Can we continue with this inquiry by seeing concepts as not-whole and leaving open the question of what *is* whole?

If so, how do we proceed to inquire? What are the means by which we can ask about the nature of life without automatically taking on an interpretation of it through some idea, teaching, philosophy, or belief?

We have already started. We have discarded the known and recognized the unknown quality of our life.

Haven't we discovered the means, the perspective that will allow this discovery?

We don't know.

We start looking.

MEDITATION — THE BEGINNING OF UNDERSTANDING?

As we take this looking without knowing into the all and every-thing of our life, we discover something wondrous, a powerful clue. Wherever we look, we can see the bare actuality of what is.

This "what is" exists moment to moment, without past or fu-ture and without conceptualization or interpretation. Even if this "what is" is itself a concept, when we view it without further ideation, it stands clear of the entanglement of our web of thought.

This is pretty exciting stuff. We are so excited we start think-ing about how exciting it is and who to tell and—poof—so much for viewing without thinking. Soon we are viewing and think-ing, then just plain thinking. Where did all that clarity go?

We had the one clue. We started looking without knowing. It was really clear and then it got really confused again.

It must be that we need more than a clue. We need a system. We need access to this clarity. We need to get there when we want to or when we need to. We need to practice. We need to meditate.

That's it—meditation. There are classes, teachers, books. This is technology and we like technology.

We catch ourselves. Wait a minute. We need to look without knowing. What is this meditation?

Let's look at it—without knowing. Is it possible to inquire into the nature of meditation itself?

We think perhaps meditation is something that gets our

minds quiet. Doesn't meditation create a kind of spaciousness or awareness so we can see what there is when there is no thought? Doesn't meditation make us more loving and happy? There are secret meditations, tantric meditations, ancient meditations, Eastern meditations, Western meditations. It's a bit daunting.

How does meditation work, and who is doing it if the mind is silent? Will meditation change us or will we just know more about our problems?

We know that meditation is supposed to help us experience the whole, somehow. But we don't know how to meditate or how meditation is supposed to work.

So now we need to understand meditation. We have to look into meditation. Perhaps we will discover that meditation is a portal to the whole, the beginning of understanding. We don't know.

PART TWO

MEDITATIONS

ON

MEDITATION

MEDITATION—WHAT IT IS, WHAT IT ISN'T, AND HOW IT GOT THAT WAY

The seeker asked the Zen master, "What is the meaning of life?"

The master replied, "Silence."

The seeker considered this for a moment, and then asked, "How do I find silence?"

The master replied, "Meditation."

"And what," the seeker asked, "is meditation?"

And the master answered, "Silence."

NEWS, WEATHER, AND MEDITATION — BROUGHT TO YOU BY DIET COKE

Meditation is not sitting for an hour with legs crossed and knees aching, wondering how long it will be until it is over.

Meditation is not the endless jabbering of the mind, unwilling to be stilled except by the brute force of will or the assertion of mantra or image.

Meditation is not the prayer to a deity, the projection of subjective states of mind onto a subjective world.

This is what we have been taught meditation is, but it is not.

Meditation is not what countless priests of countless religions have taught us.

This is a strong statement, but one only has to look to the nature of the mind to understand how we have gone so far astray.

Our minds developed as mechanisms of survival. We have survived as a species because our minds are able to anticipate and project into the near and long-term future. We are able to out-"think" other animals by modeling in our inner mental world the actuality of the outer physical world. In our hunter-gatherer days, we could project the time it would take to cross the open savannah, the likely events that would occur during the crossing, the weapons we might need, the food and water we might find in the distant forest.

To add to our relative brilliance, we developed language that began to express this modeling capacity. Now we could communicate our inner model of the outer world with someone else. We could discuss the model, agree to it, change it, fight over it.

When the rain comes, there is a loud sound and light flashes.

Language, which at first was a direct representation of our inner experience of the outer world, eventually developed into symbols and metaphors. What was once a concrete correlate of the world, reflected in the sense perceptions, became abstract.

When the rain gods are angry, the rain comes, the gods make bright flashes and loud sounds.

Over time and with the development of society and cultures, we have collectively slipped into the abstract world of language and thought. We now exist primarily in a symbolic or metaphoric world.

Today's weather, brought to you by Diet Coke, will be partly cloudy with a warming trend leading into a great weekend for relaxing in the sun. Sky5 Doppler radar tells us it will be dry and sunny with mild winds out of the southwest, a high of eighty-three degrees and a low of sixty-two. The five-day forecast is warm and dry, but with chance of rain toward the end of the week, so get out there now and have some fun.

Our world has become cluttered with ideas, symbols, projections, and pressures. The weather is no longer what is occurring in our environment. It is sponsored by a company that wants to sell us something. It is brought to us by a media source that wants to convince us of its own importance. We must process complex pseudoscientific projections of the coming days and anticipate our needs relative to those projections. Above all, we must have fun before it is too late and it starts raining. And we haven't even had our morning coffee yet.

This is the world we inhabit when we first hear the word *meditation.* In this cluttered world, meditation is a symbol. It is not actual. We hear the word and we speak the word, but the word does not represent anything concrete. It represents something else.

Meditation as Metaphor

If we can understand what meditation represents, what its metaphoric meaning is, we can understand clearly what its actuality is and what it isn't.

Meditation comes to us prepackaged. Just as the weather is sponsored by Diet Coke and Channel 5, meditation is brought to us by something. When we get the weather from Diet Coke, we are not just getting the weather, we are also getting Diet Coke. Meditation is brought to us by a religion, a philosophy, a school of psychology. It is brought to us by a teacher, an advocate, a translator. It comes to us in a context. It comes to us with a projection of the future, the end result of practicing the meditation. It comes with instructions and an outcome.

We take on meditation because we want what it promises. We want the outcome.

Meditation symbolizes the result. We take on meditation practice because we expect results, and meditation promises them.

Today's Snake Oil

Symbolic meditation practice may promise all kinds of things, but it is snake oil.

If we think we should be peaceful, we find a meditation that promises bliss. This meditation symbolizes the end of our agitation.

If we think we should be aware, we find a meditation that promises mindfulness. We project a world of attentive wisdom out of our distracted minds.

If we want power, we find a meditation that promises psychic phenomena or manifestations of our desires. If we want faith, we find a meditation that assures us closeness to God.

This is not meditation. This is our self, our mind, projecting, modeling, surviving. Our minds have the capacity to create unlimited experiences. Prepackaged meditation gives us the experience we want, the results we are promised. We will absorb it all in our increasingly cluttered minds.

We don't care if we take on medieval cultures from halfway around the world when we take on our meditation—the more exotic, the more foreign, the better.

We don't mind bowing, supplicating, compromising our own intelligence. We love using foreign words as if we understood their esoteric meanings. We find comfort in abandoning our own rituals and taking up rituals from a distant culture, imbuing these practices with the meaning we could never find at home. We look the other way at the abuses of power coming from our teachers. We are, after all, meditating, and when we are done— and it may be several thousand lifetimes before we are through— we will have whatever it is we were promised. We are sure of it. As we sit and meditate, the pain in our legs and backs assures us that something wonderful must be happening.

The Knowing Look of
the Senior Meditation Student

What, exactly, is happening when we meditate?

We are scared, confused, and mostly overwhelmed by our lives. We rebelled. We started looking around for some answers.

We come across confident-looking people who tell us that we don't have to be scared, confused, and overwhelmed. Some of these confident people are religious authorities and some are secular. They teach methodologies of meditation. We are tired of trying to figure it out on our own and so we plug in to a method. We now have a map, an explanation, and perhaps even some theology. We have a group of friends who share our beliefs. We can rest.

One of the things that we discover about meditation is that it is hard to do what the instructor teaches. It is hard to sit still. The mind is never quiet. We are not really sure if we are visualizing correctly. We forget to repeat our mantra and we start thinking about the grocery shopping.

We have the actuality of our condition, but we also have the description of what it should be. We experience that juxtaposition as conflict and pressure. We should be more like the description and less like what we are. We are disturbed by this. We see others who are senior students and who have the knowing look of someone who is living the description. That is impressive. We become more determined.

We want to have the described state of mind and so, eventually, we just create it. We shove our scared, confused, and over-whelmed self down into the dark recesses of our being and take on the bright new world of meditation. We can now have the knowing look and can describe the ever-deepening experiences. We have arrived. But where?

We haven't liberated ourselves. We have simply created a new, metaphoric level of symbolism and confusion in our lives. We don't show our conflict, but it is there. We know it because it is still agitating us down in the bowels of our being.

The Crashing Silence of Giving Up

Our meditation doesn't help us. Our rituals don't help us. Our adopted esoteric language doesn't help us. We have tried so many ways of resolving our conflicts, but we know we are still con-flicted.

When all the clutter is stripped away, we are left with the ac-tuality of our mind and body, with no interpreter, no help, and no way out. We sit there in the shock of the realization that every-thing we have tried to do has been useless and everything we are trying to understand is out of reach.

In the spontaneity of that moment, in the crashing silence of our mind giving up, we experience the first moment of medita-tion. We have started to investigate meditation without belief, without a cultural overlay, without ritual.

Meditation, we discover, is not something we do but some-thing that is.

TECHNIQUES FOR
EXPLORING THE MIND

Who Thought All of This Up?

Meditation is defined by the dictionary as the act of reflection, contemplation, focusing one's thoughts or projecting within the mind, but in colloquial use the term is used very loosely and describes everything from practices of neoshamanism to Christian prayer.

No matter what the context, there are several broad categories of meditation training. Concentration techniques train the mind to focus on a sound, an image, a word (mantra), an external object, or on some body sensation. These methods quiet the mind by engaging it in repetition. Those who practice these techniques report effects including states of tranquility and enhanced psychic states.

Meditation techniques that are designed to increase awareness take a different approach to the mind. These techniques often combine concentration methods with suggested ways of increasing attention to body/mind phenomena and sensory stimuli. This can mean quieting the external environment or slowing down the activity level so there is less to attend to as well as training the mind to pay attention to, but not analyze, what we experience.

Devotional meditation and prayer are not concerned with restructuring our relationship to our minds but focus on our relationship to a deity or the cultivation of qualities of love, devotion, and surrender. Devotees may simply worship or ask for intercessions, help, or healings. Every world religion has rituals related to its deity and theology, and practices designed to create the proper state of mind for its believers.

Each of these types of meditation—concentration, awareness, and devotion—has a framework of ideology to support it, instructions, practices, and expected results. Within the limitation of the type of technique, the meditations often work: concentration meditation does tend to focus the mind; awareness meditation does tend to increase watchfulness; devotional practices do create feelings of love. Each type of meditation inspires results. But there are always conditions on these results and side effects from them.

It is helpful to remember, as we voyage into the vast universe of meditation and all that it will reveal to us, that we are often walking on well-trodden ground. We may lose our perspective and forget that fact. We may take someone else's description of his or her experience for our experience. We may confuse our potential for our current actuality.

This problem is exacerbated not just by the romanticism of spiritual literature and the mythology of long-dead teachers but particularly by living teachers who are happy to guide us through their experience to their end—and often *for* their end and benefit. We may go along on this conceptualized inner journey as if it were our own. The human mind loves to follow, especially when it will be rewarded for its allegiance with power, certainty, or security.

If we are interested in a life of discovery and if we are interested in meditation as an expression of that life, then the experience of someone else, no matter how fantastic, is useful only as a cross-reference to our own experience. As coexplorers of the universe we can compare notes, check out the specimens and samples that we have collected, and examine the maps and journals that we have assembled.

But looking at the map is not the same as going down the river. Examining a specimen is not the same as observing the life form in its habitat. Hearing, and even believing, another explorer's adventure is not the same as having our own.

We have our own adventure to undertake.

So when we read or listen to any description of meditation, or spiritual experience, first let us understand that we have to find out what is true, through our own direct perception.

Sometimes a spiritual teaching is not even the experience of the teacher, but of another teacher or even a book that the teacher encountered. The teacher has substituted this secondhand knowledge for his or her own experience and is teaching it. This teaching can refer back to endless chains of spiritual plagiarism without anyone even realizing that nobody knows who really thought it all up. The teaching goes on as if it were coming from the immediacy of the teacher's experience, but, in fact, these experiences are imaginary.

The mind can create a virtual reality almost indistinguishable from actuality. As students of such a teacher, we can only learn virtual reality. If what we are looking for is actuality, we are profoundly lost.

THE CULTURAL WRAPPINGS
OF SPIRITUAL TEACHINGS

A spiritual student tends to accept unconsciously the cultural wrappings that most spiritual teachings come in. There are very few teachers who have fully understood their own culture's effect on them. Their personalities and expressions are culturally dictated. Their spirituality is contextual and commonplace in their own society, whereas for us it is exotic and vastly more interesting than our own spiritual or religious heritage.

Exotica isn't the issue, however. The problem is that we unconsciously take on the teacher's cultural paradigm along with its inconsistencies when we take on the teaching. Suddenly we are using another language, another diet, another way of dressing and interacting. We are observing holidays that have no history for us, accepting deities that have no inherent qualities for us, taking names that are often downright silly, and accepting behavior in our newly adopted culture that we would never have put up with before. We have no idea why we are doing this or even *that* we are doing it. Or do we know what we are doing, but choose to look the other way?

We have replaced one set of social conditioning with another. We have swapped one set of friends for another. We aren't absorbing spiritual teaching. We are absorbing behavioral modification.

If a teaching isn't free of its own cultural wrappings, how can it give expression to freedom, to the universal?

THE LIMITATION OF MEDITATION SYSTEMS

Meditation technology, in and of itself, is a wonderful and tremendously important aspect of our collective knowledge. This information on how to access and modify areas of our mind has been developed and refined over thousands of years and uncountable hours of inner exploration and experimentation.

Techniques of meditation can put us in contact with parts of our reality and can increase our sense of stability, spaciousness, and concentration. These techniques can change the way our bodies function and can enhance our health and vitality; they can bring order and meaning to our lives.

This is something. But it is not enough.

Meditation techniques cannot take us beyond our selves, beyond the self-centered identity that distorts the benefits that accrue from our practices. A better "me," a more spacious, aware, concentrated "me," is still an entity existing for and about itself. That better "me" is still existing in isolation, division, and conflict.

This core issue cannot be approached nor can it be resolved by meditation techniques, which, after all, are being practiced by the core issue itself, by "me."

We can do absolutely nothing about this "me." Doing nothing is not a technique. It can neither be taught nor learned. It cannot be practiced. The paradoxical hopelessness of the "me" realizing its own nature leaves us without an option, without a response, without a method. This stillness, without the possibility of action, without the hope for redemption, is the spontaneous realization of the truth of life.

We can't make it happen. We can't prepare for it. We can't learn it.

There is no mediation required, no interpretation needed. We are already there, all the time, without effort.

No meditation technique will help, no matter how powerful it is, no matter how diligent we are about our practices. The question is, How much help do we need in getting to where we are?

From where we are, from the silence of the moment, we can make use of the technologies of meditation. Now we are not trying to get somewhere. We are not trying to become better. We are not looking for power.

We can use meditation techniques as tools of exploration, the means of inquiry into the structures of our universe. Techniques have their usefulness, and they have their limitations.

Exploring the Mind

To make use of meditation techniques as tools of exploration, rather than religious rituals or belief systems, requires humility.

We are fascinated with the notion of understanding. We are sure the knowledge that we have accumulated through a lifetime of learning is very, very important.

It isn't.

It is very, very much in the way of direct perception. What we already know is static, but the life we seek to understand is not.

The hubris of knowledge must be the first sacrifice. For it, we get nothing in return. Nothing is a great gift indeed. Humility can occur in us, but, of course, we can never really know that we are humble because then we would become quite proud of our accomplishment.

Oliver Wendell Holmes suggested that humility was the primary of all virtues—for other people. It is certainly too unprotected and uncertain a place to reside for us. Humility is the absence of a particular position in relation to the world around us, the silencing of the critic within, the surrender to the movement of life without interpretation.

Without humility, the use of meditative technologies will not bring about anything other than the accumulation of more information. We may know more about our minds, the reality in which we exist, and the effects of certain practices, but our life will never be transformed when all we are doing is accumulating more experiences.

What if, on the other hand, we become explorers of a new world? Now as we approach our mind, our body, our energies, and the interactions with the world around us, meditation becomes a fresh and useful tool. We are not meditating out of expectation or for a result, but rather we are totally open to the actuality of what we touch.

What we touch is ourselves. What we experience is the experiencer. We are the world we are investigating, the meditation we are meditating.

In the fable of the blind men and the elephant, each man held a part of the elephant and could describe with great certainty what he experienced. The man who held the tail described a snakelike animal. The man who held the leg described an animal that grew straight and tall like a tree. The man who touched the trunk felt the strength of a giant, gripping appendage. None of the men could see the totality, and each was convinced that what he could experience was certainly the whole.

All the forms of meditation can give us a glimpse of aspects of our world, but no technique will help us see the entirety. This is because the mind, the experiencer, is blind to itself. The experiencer, the core sense of self, divides the whole into aspects and is certain that the aspect is the whole.

Meditation can tell us a great deal about the tail, or the leg, or the trunk of the elephant. This is useful information. But only humility can remind us that we are blind, and that the whole elephant will never be in our grasp.

CONCENTRATION MEDITATION— THE SCARECROW GOES TO THE WIZARD FOR A BRAIN

THE SEER AND THE YOGI

The seer came to the riverbank where a yogi had been practicing his occult powers of concentration for many decades.

"What realization have you come to?" asked the seer.

The yogi replied, "I have come to a great power. After many years of repeating my secret mantra and performing many austerities, I can now walk on water."

The yogi demonstrated his amazing capacity by crossing the river, placing one foot after the other on top of the water.

"Ah, your years of effort are worth only a rupee," said the seer.

"What do you mean?" exclaimed the yogi.

In reply, the seer said, "You see that boatman? He will take me across the river for just a rupee."

Spiritual mythology reports that concentration techniques can give us great powers of clairvoyance, the ability to fly, levitate, or dematerialize. This is very exciting, and we should all be very interested in these possibilities.

But these potentials are largely the products of the literature of spiritual romanticism, unscrupulous magic tricks, the psychology of mass hysteria, spiritual marketing, and hearsay. There is practically nothing that is both documented and objectively verified that convincingly demonstrates such powers. There are, however, numerous anecdotal accounts of personal observations and experiences of such extraordinary capacities. Subjectively one may experience these phenomena as actual.

Let us even assume for the moment that meditation techniques do allow us to access otherwise untapped human potentials. The question still remains whether these powers are related in any way to the fundamental issues that need to be resolved in our life. Magical powers do not produce happiness, equanimity, or rest. Often the appearance of these capacities—whether imaginary or not—is simply a distraction from our basic inquiry and one more acquisition of a still-hungry ego.

The nature of these mental powers is subjective. These powers are in the field of thought, which is within reality or the known. They cannot take us outside this limited, personal world, although these abilities may give us a measure of control within the relative world.

If control or manipulation of reality is what we are after, this is a way to it. It is a long way, and in the end we may find that what we discover is worth only a rupee.

FEAR AND LOATHING ON THE SPIRITUAL PATH

As we embark on the path of power, there is something we can discover quickly, something that requires little effort and is quite valuable. It is the nature of our motivation. What is the reason for our drive for control over our environment? Why do we seek the security, the surety of a world that we create and control, but in which we may have no relationship to anything but our own minds?

This basic question about ourselves and the expression of our life can never be addressed by the concentration of mind, the manipulation of relative states of consciousness, or the power that results from a focused mind. The question is simply not addressed by these mind-training meditation techniques and the teachings that surround them.

Our drive for power and control comes from the deep fear with which we often experience our lives. This fear is a lack of security and is the core of our survival instincts. Fear is the constant alertness to potential danger. It is animalistic in nature. In the natural world, fear is biologically based. In the human, it has become conceptual, habitual. Fear has become the subliminal backdrop to much of our life and our society. Fear exists without morality, it is ruthlessly competitive, it has no relationship to anything.

We are driven by fear but seldom acknowledge it. In our search for power and control, it is fear that has power and that controls us. We fear, and we loathe our fear.

Without fear, we have no need for power.

But we do have fear, and since we fear, we look for something, anything, that will give us security. We take on concentration meditation because we are told that it will still our mind and help us control our world. We are given a mantra—sometimes it is a secret mantra—that is supposedly imbued with special powers.

54

We diligently repeat the mantra, hoping to focus our world and find peace.

We believe we will find security, but will we? Is a mind that has been bludgeoned into a focused state really still? What has happened to our confusion, our conflict, our mental chaos in the process of concentration?

The conflicts in our life have not disappeared. We have focused our mind, we may even have learned to control certain levels of our mind. But in the process we have dulled ourselves. We have destroyed the receptiveness of one of our senses. The mind is our window on reality. Without it we can neither function nor can we apprehend the world around us.

Our relationships are still confusing. Our finances are still in shambles. Our health is still a challenge. And we still don't have a clue about our life.

We do have a very focused mind and perhaps even some very interesting inner experiences. There even may be physiological changes in our brain and brain chemistry. We may feel different from how we felt before.

But unless we walk away from the meditation practice, or integrate it with the rest of our life, we are stuck. We are not better off and stuck. We are worse off and stuck.

Those who came to concentration meditation to relieve their psychological pain have found a sedative. It works, but with the sedation comes fogginess, sleepiness, loss of contact.

The sedative works just as well for those who came to concentration meditation not just to relieve their pain but to understand the very nature of pain. Sedating meditation also tells a lot about the nature of the mind. It is time to move on and go deeper into this nature.

The value of concentration meditation is that it gives us a bit more space in our mental world, it gives us some focus of thought, and it gives us temporary relief from stress and tension. There is a distinct mind/body response to the simplification of our mind activity. This is valuable to explore and may allow us to access unknown areas of our beings.

But let's not make a habit of it.

The mind's nature is that it becomes addicted to the concentration and unable to integrate the movement of feeling, thought, and perception. The flow of thought becomes antithetical to the concept of peace. The activity of the world becomes a threat. Relationships can become a disturbance.

The mind, once habituated to activity, is now habituated to the dullness of a singular focus. The practitioner no longer walks down the street but walks down the street doing his mantra. The practitioner's world is viewed through the mantra. It becomes the mantra. It cannot exist without the mantra.

When we walk away from this world and do so without taking our mantra with us, we are plunged into the chaos again. And yet it is a refreshing chaos. It is vital. It is not dead and dull, distanced by a mind technique designed to keep us from feeling anything.

Our life is back. It is full of conflict and difficulty. But we are present and in contact with our life.

Manic Concentration and Samadhi

Years ago there was a meditation system taught by a manic teacher who insisted that concentrating the mind was the key to the universe. His students would sit with absolute alertness during his meditation sessions, because he walked around with orchestra cymbals and crashed them behind your head if you looked as though you were slumping or losing your focus. He would shout, "Concentrate, concentrate! It only takes a few seconds of concentration for the mind to go into samadhi!"

Samadhi is the state of merger with the cosmos described in every romantic book on Indian spirituality, so the students tried very hard amidst their teacher's shouts and crashing cymbals, which were really quite nerve-jangling.

But it was like trying to grab a wet bar of soap. The harder the students tried, the more their minds seemed to slip through the grasp of their awareness. It is difficult to describe the force of crashing cymbals on the central nervous system that has achieved some relative level of rest.

There is no evidence that anyone ever did get to samadhi with this teacher, although he was quite a charismatic individual with his fire and focus, his wild-eyed fervor. He later died of a heart attack.

Simple Exercises in
Concentration Meditation

Concentration meditation is easy to experience as a negative, that is, it is easy to see how unfocused our minds are. Sit, close your eyes, and pay attention to any one thing—a golden diamond you visualize, the sound of the mystic Om as you chant it over and over, or your own breath as it enters and leaves the tip of your nostrils. You can sit on a chair, sit in a yogic position, or lie on your bed. Focus your mind on any of these things and watch it go in every other direction but the one you intend for it. Concentration meditation is simple if you want to experience the actuality of your mind, as it is, not as you would like it to be. Trying to focus your mind is a wonderful introduction to its mercurial nature.

But concentration meditation is not about actuality, it is about concentration. It attempts to train the mind to remain still and focused on one object. To do this requires great effort, patience, and a little bit of brutality.

Try the concentration meditation again, but this time, forget about where your mind goes when you try to focus it. Just bring it back to the object of concentration—the diamond, the sound, the breath, or whatever you are using.

Do this for fifteen minutes. It is very hard. Diamond. Diamond. Daydream. Whoops. Diamond. Diamond. Bills to be paid. What about dinner? Whoops. Diamond. Diamond. And so forth.

What's the point of this? The point is supposed to be that

when you have trained your mind just to see a diamond, and when nothing else is occurring, your state of consciousness is altered.

Through concentration we can strive for an unobtainable state that we can get to through hardship, and by means of methods described to us by someone who claims to be there. Once there, we will be different. Once we are different, we can be the one who is teaching this, motivating others to go through the hardship. We can be the one who is presumed to be there, wherever that is.

Meanwhile, we are left sitting, thoughts wandering, as we struggle to concentrate a mind that has no intention of sitting still.

Most of us have never experienced our minds focused in a singular fashion, and most of us never will.

SIDE EFFECTS OF CONCENTRATION MEDITATION — DON'T TRY THIS AT HOME

If we are persistent with our mind, we can wrestle it into some kind of relative submission. We can concentrate on a single object, thought, sound, or whatever. Side effects can be pleasant or unpleasant.

On the pleasant end of the spectrum, once we get past the struggle and get our minds beaten into submission, the body tends to relax. This is very pleasant, and most new meditators simply fall asleep at this point. There is nothing wrong with a little nap, except it's not very spiritual and, of course, we lose what little concentration we were able to muster and are now spinning off into fantasy land.

Eventually we learn to concentrate, relax, and not fall asleep. This is even more pleasant, and consequently we usually get pulled into the whole experience. Sometime later we come out of it with the realization that we haven't been asleep, and we haven't lost our concentration, but we lost any awareness of the whole show. We have sunk into a no-man's-land of unconscious torpor. The mind is concentrated, the body is awake, but nobody's home.

This is an interesting state, actually, but again, not spiritually valued, and the problem is that we can't really describe it to our friends, because we were all torpored out. But at least we didn't start snoring. There is no one more wretched in a meditation group than the one who falls asleep *and* snores.

This is about as far as it gets for the person who is meditating for an hour or two a day. Most of us will have to go into a retreat setting where we can sit for longer periods of time without distraction to get into the good stuff.

Beyond Torpor and into the Good Stuff

Real go-getters will push past lethargy in their meditation and finally get concentrated, stay awake, and stay aware. This could take twenty years of practicing, or going through long retreat periods, but we are having fun, and getting quite a lot of napping done on the way. Now we are in a very sublime place and, indeed, a very interesting place. Unfortunately it is usually not a very pleasant place.

As it turns out, all this falling asleep had a purpose, which was to avoid what happens when we concentrate our minds and don't fall asleep. Often all the psychic garbage we have been storing in our minds and bodies begins to emerge at this point, unsolicited, unwanted, and mostly unrestrained. The faucet has been turned on, and out gushes stuff. This is usually disagreeable, and considered by many to be a bit frightening.

Out of the mind can pour lights, sounds, visions, monsters, gods/goddesses, precognitions; you name it and it is there somewhere. And if we don't have a particular vision or experience, our minds can order it up from the collective unconsciousness. Suddenly we're getting into past lives, future lives, somebody else's lives, languages we never learned, places we've never heard of, planets, hells, heavens, yowie zowie . . . what is all this stuff? Sometimes there are physical manifestations such as body jerking, swellings, marks, heat, cold, feelings of pressure, and so forth. There could be manifestations of various illnesses, fluctuating energy/fatigue levels, loss or amplification of sexual appetites, and sleep disturbance (which makes us very happy to have gotten those naps in).

The few practitioners who actually get to this kind of experience (and don't just read about it and talk about it) will mostly get stuck here. They might be repulsed by the whole thing and decide that it is really a good time to go back to school and get that master's of social work and really do something worthwhile with their lives. Other meditators are very attracted to all the fire-works and hoopla and will spend the rest of their days generating and watching the show and, of course, telling anyone who will listen all about it. Some people cannot integrate these kinds of ex-periences. They become destabilized and will end up seeking psychological help to put their former world back together again.

The spiritual literature is full of descriptions of what this stuff is and what to do about it. At the risk of adding one more com-mentary to an already overdiscussed area, the suggestion here would be to do nothing about any of this. It's interesting, but so is television. The intrinsic value is about equivalent to television.

Without acting on or reacting to the material of the psyche, whatever it may appear to be, we can actively observe it and at the same time be free of its hooks. In this way, we get to under-stand something of the nature of our world, but we don't get lost in it. This quality will see us through the fireworks. Then things get a bit quieter.

After moments, days, years, or decades, the manifestations subside, the mind/body gets quiet, and it's a little hard to explain why, but generally at that point there is nothing much more ap-pealing than a good nap. This is a very spiritual nap. It is even okay to snore.

WHAT IS THIS STUFF, ANYWAY?

The stuff that comes up in our mind when we are doing pro-longed meditation can be really exciting. It is everything we ever imagined the spiritual life would be like. In fact it is actually, precisely, everything we ever imagined. It is imagination. It is thought generating more of its forms.

These thought weavings are fascinating. One could take a life time to study them. For those who have dedicated a great part of their lives to experiencing these kinds of phenomena there is some solace in this fascination. There is something gratifying in finding that there are thought forms that are far more interesting than the mundane thoughts with which we occupy our lives.

Understanding all of the permutations of thought is a skill. Getting to this deep level of experience is an achievement. Being a person who is able to do this is highly unusual. But the ultimate truth does not lie in this realm, only relative truth resides here. Those unusual few who achieve this skill and do not understand its limitation are stuck. They cannot find freedom, they cannot find love, they cannot find rest.

Those who find this sublime world of wonder and get caught there usually end up as spiritual teachers. They teach us how to find our way to Wonderland. They can show us the way there, but they cannot show us the way out.

AWARENESS MEDITATION—
PAY ATTENTION,
THIS IS IMPORTANT

THE GOOD THING ABOUT CONCENTRATION

Concentration is a useful mental tool. It is helpful as a means to relax the body and bring our minds to some relative order. In combination with awareness, it is a potent vehicle for the exploration of the psyche. It is invaluable in our day-to-day functions as a means of focusing our energy in a particular direction or on a particular project.

Concentration is a good tool, but, like all tools, it is good for some tasks and not for others.

Concentration won't do us any good if we are not aware of what we are concentrating on, or even that we are concentrated. Awareness is a very important component of the quest for enlightenment. Without it we wouldn't realize we were realized, and then what good would realization do us?

Without awareness, Jesus would have been a mediocre carpenter with a lot of Band-Aids on his hands; the Buddha would have succumbed to the temptations during his last-stand meditation at Bodh Gaya and become just another wandering sadhu, albeit with lots of interesting powers. Without awareness, there are no saints, prophets, or founders of religions.

AWARENESS IS HIP

Awareness is very hip and it's hard to argue with its importance. There are awareness classes, awareness exercises, and even vitamins and herbs that are touted as awareness enhancers.

Awareness is a buzzword in spiritual circles. Everyone thinks that he or she should have it. Most want more of it than they have. Some lose it on a regular basis but find it again. Everyone knows someone who has lost it permanently. A few claim to have found it permanently, and they usually teach other people how to get it. Those who become students of awareness are people who don't have it, or who lost it, or who heard about it and want it, or were just bored and wandered into the presentation.

Awareness is so much a part of the spiritual scene that we have *lost* awareness. We have forgotten that awareness is a word, that it has become jargon, that it has come to symbolize our sense of lack more than a state of consciousness. We are not going to awareness class to find awareness. We are going because we *are* aware. What we are aware of is that we are unhappy.

It is not that our lives are disasters. We are not the sort that complains that our lives are fragmented, painful, meaningless, and, to top it off with an ironic twist, far too short. There are some people whose marriages are floundering, whose managed-care doctor tells them not to worry about the lumps but won't refer them to the specialist to make sure. These people have credit cards that are maxed out. They're lactose intolerant.

Most of us are not that.

Most of us are just not satisfied with our lives.

But unhappiness is no longer hip. It's been tried. It doesn't market well. Prozac is in. Depression is out. Depressed people do not produce as much or as fast. Depression-related losses to businesses cost billions of dollars each year. Depressed people are a drag to be around.

Starbucks Coffee is paying attention to this attention craze. They started selling awareness by the cup to otherwise depressed and rain-soaked Seattle dwellers and became such a success that even Wall Street paid attention. Seattle woke up. Grunge music faded. Desperate unhappiness faded. Starbucks went public, and paying attention became a growth industry.

Marketing firms track awareness. Which brand comes to mind first? What association occurs with what brand and does that relate to the targeted market segment? How many people are paying attention to the ads during the Super Bowl and how many have run off to the bathroom?

Awareness is big business. And awareness is big in the spiritual world, too. Awareness learning centers are popping up all over the United States.

In both the Buddhist and Yogic meditation traditions, concentration meditation is a beginning practice that eventually allows the practitioner to settle down enough so that he or she can be aware of what is going on. These Eastern meditation systems have very thorough descriptions of techniques to develop awareness, all of which require a certain amount of concentration of mind.

Awareness meditation, based on these Eastern systems, is one of the fastest-growing practices in the West due in part to its simplicity and in part to the fact that the practitioner gets quick results, even if the results are negative. Awareness meditation is simple. It requires little more than endless sitting and paying attention. It teaches simple awareness exercises that unavoidably show how unaware we are. The results are "negative," but they are instant.

In the beginning, students are taught to develop concentration, usually through attention to the breath. Some teachers then tell the meditator to begin to cultivate awareness through noting what is occurring in each moment, without evaluating it, without liking it or disliking it. It goes something like this: breathing, sensation in nostril, tickling, aversion to tickling, thought arises to scratch, thought passes away, pain in knee, thought about lunch, pain in shoulder, and so forth and so on.

The noting process gets more refined, with the practitioner noting intentions to take actions. In some systems the practitioner slows down the physical processes of daily activity, living in slow motion so that the detail of that activity can be observed. Eventually the noting process falls away and the meditator is aware of the body/mind phenomenon without internal verbalization. This has the quality of a stream of moment-to-moment awareness of various thoughts, feelings, and sensations.

This is just the beginning of awareness meditation.

Consciousness 101 — Exercises in Awareness

1. Take a comfortable seat either in a straight-backed chair or cross-legged on a cushion. Close your eyes and pay attention to the breath entering and exiting your nostrils. Don't move during this meditation. Begin to note everything that takes place: thoughts, emotions, physical sensations, external sounds. Just notice them. Don't necessarily interpret them. You don't need to evaluate the good or bad, the painful or pleasurable. But if you do start evaluating, then note that. After noting, bring your attention back to your breath. Do this for thirty minutes.

2. Take a comfortable seat as before. Pay attention to your breath until your mind becomes concentrated. Now put your awareness on your toes and move your attention very slowly, point by point, through your entire body working from your toes to the top of your head. You may only get through one leg in a sitting. Note anything that you become aware of during this process. Do this for thirty minutes.

3. Once you are able, do the exercises described above for an hour each.

4. Sit for an hour. Pay attention. Don't note. Don't pay particular attention to the breath. Don't particularly evaluate what you are experiencing. Just pay attention.

Are We Aware Yet?

Long meditation retreats can bring about great focus, deep awareness, and expansive mental silence. In this rarified atmosphere great realizations often occur.

Then it is time to leave. The real world, the life from which the practitioner was retreating, rushes in and typically knocks the practitioner and his realization into oblivion.

Many awareness meditation practitioners adapt to this on-slaught of actuality by adopting a language and stance that distance them from their feelings. These thoughts and feelings are all empty. All phenomena are impermanent. Life is pain. These are the truisms extracted from Eastern meditative traditions. They sound good. They have a certain internal logic and a whole body of philosophy to back them up. And when the checkbook is empty and the landlord tells you that you are indeed imperma-nent, then life *is* a pain. The problem is that there are a lot of people who practice awareness rather than putting their life in order.

Other practitioners buffer themselves from their lives by creating a watcher. This is the one who is aware of the mess that is going on all around. The watcher is not the body, but it is aware of the body. The watcher is not the mind. It is aware of the mind. It is not the thoughts, feelings, sensations. It is aware of all of these things. The watcher is a big trap in awareness meditation. The meditator has been trained to watch everything, except the watcher. The watcher cannot be watched. This is a paradox and a big, big problem if you are trying to get enlightened.

If you are just trying to get by in life, the watcher is okay. You'll never have to get hurt again. You'll never have to take any risks again. You'll never have to take any responsibility again. All you have to do is watch. It is the solution to everything. It is the greatest thing since low-fat tofu.

Once you are watching your life, you won't have to live it. You are aware. Or that is what you've convinced yourself. The reality is that the mind has created a safe place to be while the body re-produces, ages, and dies. That's it. It does have fewer side effects than psychiatric medication, but otherwise, being the watcher of your own life is inherently limited, no matter what the rationale is.

Most awareness meditators get stuck at the watcher. Convinced that they have arrived, they walk around with a fixed gaze and watch. They suggest to their friends the efficacy of practice. They read English translations of obscure sutras. Whenever they can, they practice watching by sitting still on a cushion—and watching. Or perhaps it is watching themselves sitting on a cushion.

For those who are not content watching, there is more.

What is next is an extensive blueprint of stages of meditation, states of mind, levels of understanding, and depths of awareness. Like an onion being peeled away, layer after layer, the mind of the practitioner is revealed. Light flows where once there was a mind; reality is seen as continuous and discontinuous; the watcher collapses; the drive to enlightenment strengthens, then it too collapses; effort falls away; the practice itself falls away; various levels of buddhahood occur; then final enlightenment.

Where are we? We seem to be enlightened, which was the point of all of this. We are very happy about that in an empty sort of way. Well, maybe when we are enlightened we can be happy in a full way, since we recognize that it's all empty anyway.

Its all exciting, except for the fact that we aren't exactly there, we're here and we're listening to or reading a description translated from Pali or Tibetan written many hundreds of years ago. We're probably not going to spend years or a lifetime in meditation retreats, we're going to spend a few weekends.

This is a big problem.

We have confused our direct experience in our actual lives

with a beautiful and intricate philosophy from the distant past. We don't know if we are experiencing something or if we simply believe we should be experiencing something.

Are we aware or do we just believe we are aware?

How to Be in the Moment

How can I be in the moment?

You are in the moment. Where else is there?

But I'm not aware all the time.

Well, where are you, then?

No, aware, not where.

If you aren't aware, then where are you?

I'm off in thoughts and fantasies.

So?

That's not awareness. Awareness is in the moment.

How do you know you aren't in the moment?

I'm off in thoughts and fantasies.

How do you know you're off in thoughts and fantasies?

I become aware that I'm there.

Where?

No, aware.

You're aware.

Yes, I'm aware that I'm not aware.

Where are you aware?

There.

When you are there, isn't that, then, here?

Okay, here.

So you are aware that you are not aware and that you are there,
which is actually here.

Precisely.

What was your question?

How can I be in the moment?

You are in the moment. Where else is there?

How to Be in the Moment after That —
What Is Awareness, Anyway?

Awareness is a word. If we stay aware of nothing else in our lives,
let us stay aware of this one thing. The word *awareness* is used to
describe, but not explain, a state of consciousness that is present
and that has the capacity to apprehend some element of reality.

This means that we cannot simultaneously be aware and lost
in thoughts about our childhood, although we can be aware of
the thoughts of our childhood. So awareness is present and while
thought may be an object of awareness's apprehension, awareness
does not exist in thought itself.

We can begin to see some serious difficulty in talking about
awareness. If awareness is outside of thought, it is outside of language, it is outside of reality itself. So what are schools of awareness teaching? How do you teach something that is beyond
everything that is known?

This is, of course, the dilemma. What is being taught is within
the realm of the known. What is being taught is a system of ideas.

We are not being taught meditation. We are being conditioned to conceptualize our experiences in particular ways.

It is not hard to see how this could very well get us someplace better than where we started. We started in dissatisfaction, and now we are aware of our dissatisfaction. We are choicelessly aware of our pain. This is, no doubt, better than just being in pain. Or is it?

We are walking, using our new skills as meditators, we are paying attention to the pain in our foot. Noticing pain. Noticing pain. Noticing pain. We are very happy that we have reached this choiceless awareness of our pain. We just notice it. It is just pain. This must be what enlightenment is like.

This is not enlightenment. Let's take the rock out of our shoe. Pain isn't just an object of awareness, it is also a message, a call to action, a thread that if followed leads to a deeper understanding and a deeper expression of our lives.

We are so busy being aware that we forget to live.

Awareness teachings often use a metaphor of a boat crossing the river to describe the techniques that are taught. You need awareness techniques only to cross over, and once you are on the other side you let the techniques go. But where is the other side, and what is it we are crossing? Aren't we living as we are? Does life have another shore, this place called enlightenment, where things are fundamentally different? Where is it? Can anyone directly, not metaphorically, demonstrate this other side for the benefit of the rest of us? And, if not, isn't this just one more belief system we are taking on?

What is awareness, anyway?

AWARENESS, THAT ANNOYING
TIME BETWEEN NAPS

We are back to the beginning. Awareness is a word. Beyond that, nobody knows what awareness is or what to do with it. That's the fact. Awareness is a question that cannot be answered, a silence that cannot be intruded upon, something that is not owned, controlled, or used.

We cannot learn awareness and we cannot teach it. We can try to get ourselves out of the way of it, but even that is impossible. Awareness is not hard to come by. As many times as we push it away it returns. Getting awareness is as simple as getting to where we already are.

There is nothing to practice, but practicing nothing is something we all can do. If we are not asleep, we are awake. If we are awake, we must be aware. If you can read this, you are certainly awake. The nap is over, and this annoying thing called awareness is occurring.

We can try to dull ourselves with food and drink, too much television, too much work, or a thousand other things. We can buffer ourselves from our life with our ideas, our agendas, our childish demands. But we are still where we are, we are still awake, and this annoying thing called awareness is occurring.

We can't stop it.

We can't start it.

Awareness is a fact of life.

DEVOTIONAL
MEDITATION—
IF I LOVED YOU

*Complaint is the largest tribute heaven receives and the
sincerest part of our devotion.*

—Jonathan Swift

*God does not intend that man shall have a place reserved
for him to work in, since the true poverty of spirit requires
that man shall be emptied of God and all his works, so
that if God wants to act in the soul, he himself must be in
the place in which he acts. . . .*

—Meister Eckhart

GETTING TO THE HEART OF THE MATTER

Many spiritually inclined individuals are just not that interested
in sitting around focusing their mind in anticipation of an in-
evitable outpouring of psychic phenomena. They want something with a little emotional juice to it and a meditation that is a
whole lot more accessible. For these people, the need they are expressing isn't about their minds, it's about their hearts.

The heart has become a metaphor in our language. What we
mean by the heart is the feeling of expansion, of connection, of
great emotional melting unmediated by the rational mind. These

phrases are in themselves metaphoric or symbolic and so we find it quite difficult to say what we really mean by the heart. That's all right, because the heart doesn't care what it means, it simply feels. The rational mind is bothered by and dismissive of all of this indefiniteness and would much rather see some concentration meditation going on. That's something it can understand.

But the heart wants this feeling we call devotion. Devotion is the symbol for the expression of the metaphoric heart. Many of us are drawn to devotional meditation and we don't know why. We *can't* know why and still be drawn to it. In devotion, the thinking mind, the intellect, falls silent.

The relative silence of the thinking mind that has given up is powerful, but it is still relative. In devotion, we may have quieted the intellect, but have we quieted the mind in total? The repository of deeply embedded religious and psychological imagery is still active and is perhaps strengthened by the abeyance of the intellect and the resulting fervor of devotional belief. The devotee's world is still given its meaning by the religious mind and the supporting cultural paradigm.

In the theory of devotional meditation, the feeling of love and devotion is focused on an image or concept only in the beginning of the practice. As the devotion deepens, it is suggested that the object of the love, the idea, drops away and all that is left is devotion itself, love without an object or a subject. For a few, this may even occur. For most, devotion remains tied to the imagery, theology, and philosophy of the particular belief system.

DEVOTION — THE OPIATE OF RELIGION

All major religions encompass devotional meditation as a core element of their teaching. The exoteric version of this, which is intended for the masses, is generally external and iconic, represented in scripture, painting, statuary, and architecture. Some of this moves our hearts with its astonishing beauty. But at its worst it has degenerated into rote and unimaginative replication of icons and is used to manipulate and control large populations of barely interested adherents.

Nevertheless, obvious external symbols of devotion exist for anyone within a particular religious culture to meditate on and thereby glean some feeling of devotion. In an exoteric religion, devotional meditation takes the form of ritual; programmed, collective acts repeat ad infinitum. This is the glue that holds the religious form together, and it is the manifestation of a collective, but unconscious, feeling of devotion. The rituals of religion are a kind of group devotional meditation. They are powerful expressions that facilitate liturgic continuity and sectarian definition.

It is no coincidence that the fastest-growing religions are the most dogmatically ritualistic. Ritual works. It creates a sense of connection to an entire religious history. Repetition has a calming and focusing effect on the mind, much like concentration meditation. Ritual has a beginning and an end, a time and a place, and a future when it will be performed again—five times a day, once a week on Sundays, or a few times a year on special holidays. Ritual is predictable and knowable in a world that seems largely out of our control and filled to the brim with unknowables. We crave patterns that represent the undivided whole, that expand our view, that replicate the natural world.

Rituals are these patterns. Ritual provides a place of rest for the busy mind, the broken heart, the lost soul.

But rituals cannot become conscious. We cannot become fully aware of their purpose, their origin, their meaning, and their impact. If we investigate any of our rituals, something shifts. They no longer have the same feeling or meaning.

As we look, we penetrate the social construction of not only the ritual but also the religion itself. We see that we are a part of a group that is moving together through these rituals, but that we are not in contact with each other outside of these common practices. We discover that the origins of these practices have more to do with power, politics, social cohesion, and cultural history than with the revelation of any ultimate reality.

We find that there is tremendous pressure to stay within the religious practices. The penalty for deviance results in being shunned—or in some of the more extreme, but convincing, arguments for staying with the program, our souls get earmarked for hell, our possessions are confiscated, or we are simply executed.

Our group, our ritual, our belief system will always be in separation, and consequently it will always be in conflict, with some other set of beliefs and practices. And that other system of beliefs will always be in conflict with ours. This is the problem with belief. At its core it is uncertain and protective. If we practice devotion, and this devotion is to our beliefs, we are devoting ourselves just as much to the conflict that is inherent to belief.

Loving-Kindness Meditation

From the Buddhist tradition comes a powerful meditation designed to develop the qualities of love, empathy, and kindness. The meditation focuses on generating and amplifying these qualities of mind in the individual and expanding the feelings to include all living beings.

For those who have a sense of self-hatred or who tend toward anger and criticism, this cultivation of love and acceptance can deeply affect behavior and perceptual patterns. The endpoint of meditation on loving-kindness is the expansion of healing qualities beyond the practitioner and into the whole of the universe.

It is difficult to say whether what is generated with this practice is loving and kind or whether it is an imaginary state that is reinforced by the practice of certain feelings and the repetition of words that suggest that those feelings are authentic and actual.

For the practitioner, the state of mind generated is quite powerful. For the observer, the practitioner may appear to be spaced out, disconnected, and habituated to the meditation practice in order to have the experience. Some practitioners may seem profoundly unhappy, but convinced that they are not. If we are unhappy, do we want to know it? If we are unhappy and create a feeling of love through our practice, are we what we feel, or what we don't feel?

There is no question that powerful states of feeling can be generated by this kind of practice. What is not clear is whether we can understand what these feelings are in actuality and integrate them in the fullness of our life. Often we don't even know why we are trying to create these feelings or why these feelings aren't naturally there to begin with. In the end, we may be more confused by our attempts to cultivate loving-kindness, given the complexity of the contemporary psyche.

It would be nice to believe that we could do something to be loving. Mostly we believe that we should do something, because we're not sure how to love, and this creates great pain. This underlying belief is only reinforced by "practicing" love, as if we still haven't quite gotten it yet.

IF I LOVED YOU

There is a kind of devotion that is not a meditation but simply a fact. It cannot be practiced or cultivated. It is found often in people with a simple perspective on their life and seldom in theologians and philosophers.

For these few people, the very humility of their relationship to the world around them and the faith and love with which they naturally live make their lives the very expression of devotion. They are not practicing devotion; they are not practicing meditation; they are living it.

The rest of us can sit on our cushions pleading with ourselves to love all beings, but it won't help.

We can ask God, "What would happen if I decided to love you?" We will never find out.

Most of us will need to face the falseness of our belief, the inconsistencies of our faith, the shallowness of our relationship to our life. We will need to recognize that our devotion is a negotiation with life for security and that we have taken a position outside of love, as if we were love's animator.

For most of us, devotion is an obscure and inaccessible quality that we read about in spiritual literature, ritualize in religious contexts, or act out in spiritual organizations by following the lead of others. We don't feel it. We don't live it.

In actuality, it isn't.

This recognition may introduce us to the actuality of what is.

The Christian mystics call this realization the dark night of the soul, the yogis talk about *neti, neti,* "not this, not that," the dismissal of the false. It is the recognition that the actuality of love cannot be found through devotion to what it is but by discarding what it is not. What love is will always be distorted by our ideas and images. What love is not can be found and discarded, leaving what remains—the nameless, formless actuality of universal love.

The only obstruction to love is the idea of the self. This is the very self that has declared its devotion to this love. Our devotion is in the way, because our self is in the way.

Our self does not in fact exist, our devotion does not in fact exist.

There is nothing in the way of love.

AUTHORITY AND THE
SEARCH FOR SECURITY

I did not wish to bring men to me, but to themselves . . .
my boast is that I have no followers.

—Ralph Waldo Emerson

How Can We Authenticate
a Spiritual Teacher?

Traditionally meditation teachers came from the cultures where their teaching originated. Teaching meditation required years of practice and, ultimately, the blessing of their own teacher, before a new teacher would venture out.

There are still some traditional meditation teachers in circulation today, but not as many as once existed. Traditional cultures are themselves dying out. When they are not destroyed by straightforward military invasion (such as Tibet's takeover by China), they are often victims of CNN, MTV, McDonald's, Coke, and all of the rest of America's best being exported around the globe. Few of the traditional teachers have anything but a distant childhood left in their own culture. They are Westernized and often confused by the competing forces within them and outside them.

But a new, dynamic type of spiritual teacher is emerging. These teachers are generally self-created. If they come with the blessing of a guru, it is usually a dead guru who can neither confirm nor deny their authenticity. Just look at how many America newbie gurus are dragging around pictures of Ramana Maharshi to authenticate themselves. Ramana was one of India's great saints who was known for sitting most of his life in silence and being entirely indifferent to the idea of anointing a disciple to carry on his work. He has been dead for fifty years. Yet today there are dozens of teachers who sit under his picture while they lecture. Today all you have to do to be a meditation teacher is to say that you are one.

Lineage has traditionally been a way to authenticate a teacher. This seems rational enough. We can presume that if God spoke to Moses, Moses has something to say of importance. But these days God seems to be speaking to everyone.

Those who don't have a lineage create one or, better yet, begin one. To start your own lineage, just declare yourself enlightened, and then declare your first couple of disciples enlightened and tell them to go out and teach. They will. And you will have started a lineage. Even dead people have gotten into the act by channeling through with their message.

How do we sort this out? Is God speaking to all these neo-prophets? If someone isn't a lineage holder, can he or she be authentic? Just because someone is dead, does that necessarily make him profound?

The fact is, we can't sort out this mess. There is absolutely no way to figure out what is authentic. If there is a lineage, there is an opposing lineage. Somewhere back on the family tree, two underlings of the then-current teacher had a disagreement and started competing lines. Each believed the other line was false. Just try to sort out the *authentic* Christian denomination: Catholic? Greek Orthodox? Lutheran? Quaker?

Claims that God has spoken are very common and would be impressive if it weren't for the fact that God is always saying different things to different people. God tells me that all people should wear blue. God tells you that all people should wear yellow. We've got a big problem with this God-talking-to-people thing. It doesn't work.

Channeling. There are the dead people being channeled. And there are the interdimensional beings and intergalactic beings being channeled. Let's say for a moment that these dead and otherworldly beings are out there talking through a medium. Are we supposed to be so impressed by the phenomenon that we disregard the content? Is the medium the message?

Or is the message the message? And what is the message, after all?

Look at so-called channeled material. The message is whatever we want it to be. It is all and everything. It is nothing. Channeling is not helpful to us in authenticating a teacher or much of anything else.

ALL GENERALIZATIONS ARE FALSE

American spiritual teachers are a weird breed. They love to mix psychoanalytical techniques and bodywork together with their main spiel. They do their best to meld all the major religions into their presentations. They usually charge fees for their talks, books, and other products as donations to their nonprofit foundation, which in turn supports them. They are strong marketers, or have strong marketers in their organization. They teach that effort brings results. They also teach that if we are unable to bring sufficient effort to our spiritual work, there is still grace, a kind of welfare for the spiritually impoverished. In short, they are Americans teaching American values. They haven't transcended Western materialism. They have translated our culture into spiritual jargon. They sell it. We buy it.

These are generalizations about American spiritual teachers. We know that all generalizations are false. But just because these are generalizations doesn't mean these teachers are not after us. Or at least our wallets.

What Enlightened People Do
with Their Free Time

Three famous spiritual teachers, a yogi, a monk, and a dervish met one day and challenged each other to complete honesty about their weaknesses.

The yogi said, "Although I am known for my great austerities, I must admit that despite my struggles to overcome the attraction, I still love to drink."

The monk, a bit red-faced but ready to meet the challenge, said, "I don't have any problem with liquor, but even though I've meditated and I've prayed, I still cannot keep myself from giving in to the temptation of women."

There was a long pause and finally the two confessed enlightened beings turned to the dervish, and said, "So what is your failing?"

"Well," said the dervish, "I have this awful, unstoppable urge to gossip."

———

Teachers of enlightenment tell us about cosmic consciousness. They tell us about the ethereal worlds and the vast accomplishments of the spiritual way. But they seldom tell us what they do with their spare time.

We can imagine that if we were such a being, we would arise early for our morning meditation and cappuccino. We'd kiss the spouse good-bye before beginning our rush-hour commute (which we would accept with equanimity) to the office where we would spend the day doing good works, advising people on their spiritual practices, and encouraging our devotees to continue their devotion. We would never be concerned with the mortgage on our house, the office rent, the phone bills, or where to invest the money in our 401k. These are mundane and unimportant details best left to others.

We would power-lunch with reporters eager to ask us how to solve world problems, or perhaps with other enlightened beings who happened to be passing through town. After checking back with the office staff and our voice mail for last-minute crises to avert, we would head home early in order to miss the evening traffic.

We can envision a light, wholesome dinner accompanied by witty but subtly profound conversation with our doting spouse and perhaps a few close associates. Angelic children might be seen about, but definitely not heard. They are probably helping each other with their homework or talking quietly with each other about the wonders of the spiritual life.

All is well so far. It is not hard for us to understand what life must be like for an enlightened being.

But what do we do next? Is it time for the evening news, a crossword puzzle, knitting? What about weekends and holidays? What do we do on the day after New Year's Eve when everything is closed? Shouldn't enlightened beings do something enlightened?

What do enlightened people do with their free time? And why is nobody talking about this?

Could it be that enlightened beings do catch the evening news, or rent a video, or play computer games? Could it be that they do unenlightened things? If they are like us after hours, are they really as they say they are during office hours? Maybe they can't wait to get through their profound discoursing so they can get home and finish the last chapters of that romance novel or check their stock prices on-line or call their old friends and gossip.

Maybe they are bored with their work and are thinking they are wasting their life. Maybe they regret that they never made it through graduate school. Maybe they wonder why nobody asks them how *they* are doing. Maybe they'd like permission to have a bad day once in a while. It's certainly not an easy job being enlightened—the pay may be good, but the hours are long and they really never get a chance just to relax and let go.

If the enlightened are acting like one of us, then, maybe they *are* one of us, and, then, we must be one of them. Things may be a little different than they seem in this enlightenment business.

Let's check into this with the next enlightened beings we meet. Let's find out how they're really doing—and what they do with their spare time.

If You Meet the Spiritual Teacher on the Road . . .

If you meet the Buddha on the road, kill him!
—Zen koan

Here are some questions to ask yourself and any spiritual teacher with whom you might want to study, as well as some considerations about the nature of religious authority.

Why do you need a teacher? Is there something wrong with you? Why does the teacher need you? Why does the teacher teach? Why are you a student?

Crazy wisdom teachers are crazy. They don't suffer from insanity, they enjoy it. If you are going to go with one of these, why should you complain later?

Ask about the money early and often. What finances the organization and who benefits from the inflow of money? Will you be expected to empty your bank account, liquidate your possessions, or sell flowers on the street? Do the organization's brochures suggest ways to contribute stocks, bonds, and real estate? Are Visa and MasterCard accepted? How the money works will tell you a lot about how the teacher works, or doesn't.

Ask about sex. Is it required, and by whom, with whom? Is anyone talking about this openly or is this taboo?

Talk to a senior student. How many years has this person been doing the practices? Add those years to your age and ask yourself if that is who you want to be at that point in your life.

If the teacher is a man, what man who is missing from your life (physically or emotionally) does he remind you of? If it is a woman, what missing woman does she remind you of? If this is unclear, ask your mother or father, unless they don't want to talk about it right now because they are busy, you haven't seen one of them since the divorce when you were a kid, or they happen to have died. Hint: male teacher = father figure; female teacher = mother figure.

Ask the teacher if he can change your condition permanently and directly. If he says yes, ask for it on the spot and with observers present (don't go for the tantric sex ploy here). If he says no, find out what he can do for you. If he says he can do nothing, follow up; this could be an interesting person. Ask what you can do for the teacher.

Invite teachers to your house for tea. Those who come without their entourage are the most interesting. Those who come with their entourage are at least adventuresome. Those who won't come are either too important and busy for you—and what good is that?—or they are terrified of being outside of a space that they control. There may be other explanations for their not coming, and it will be helpful to you to hear what those are.

A corollary of the tea invitation is to write to a teacher. You can say anything; it doesn't matter as long as you are sincere. See what kind of response you get. Important teachers will have an underling respond and you will be placed on their mailing list. Some will ignore you. Some will respond personally. A few will respond personally and honestly.

If the teacher is old, ask yourself if your attraction could be to his or her greater life experience that comes with time. If the teacher is young, could your attraction be to the exuberance of a person whom time has not worn down? Time itself is a great teacher, although it does end up killing all of its students.

THE ADDICTION OF SPIRITUAL AUTHORITY

Why do we have such a deep need for authority, direction, and surety in both our inner and outer worlds? It is a curious element of the human condition that we crave outer domination as a means of subjugating our inner demons. It is equally curious that we look for the spontaneous experience of love in the repetition of ritual. Or that we look for a way out of the labyrinth of our minds through the absorption of spiritual concepts or psychological ideology.

The spiritual teacher may provide us with the keys to the universe, but the universe is not locked.

We believe we cannot stand on our own. We feel we don't have the personal intensity to live without a guidebook. Our understanding is secondhand. We look to another as the authority on something on which we are already an expert—our own life.

A teacher can tell us how he did it. He can tell us how his teacher did it. He can tell us how the scriptures tell us how to do it. But nobody can truly tell us how to live or how to love.

The search for authority is a search for sedation. It is an avoidance of the inherent challenge of living. It is the capitulation of our own innate spirituality in favor of the rote reproduction of another's experience.

This search for authority is at the core of our spiritual confusion. In this search we become convinced that there is something to get and someone who will show us how to get it. Our inherent and spontaneous spiritual curiosity turns to greed as we hear the promise of supernatural riches that accompany our new guide. Each step we take with that teacher is a step closer to the realization of enlightenment, samadhi, happiness, realization of our personal savior, or whatever the implicit promise is. Each step leaves us with one more step. Each day leaves us with one more day. Each practice with one more practice. Each contribution with one more to make. We are addicted to this outer authority.

FATHER KNOWS BEST

The vast majority of spiritual authorities are men. Either men are just better at this spiritual game, they are more aggressive about getting the available positions, they actively exclude the competition, or something else is going on.

Many of us had a problematic or incomplete relationship with our fathers. Although we may understand the limitations of stereotyping gender roles, it is still often the case that the father appears as a powerful authority figure in our psyche. We are searching high and low for that father so that he can give us some assurance. We want to know that we are safe, that there is nothing in the closet, and that Santa Claus does exist. The teacher is the father.

Father knows best. The teacher knows best. We regress to an infantile vantage point where we can accept simple solutions to unmanageable problems. Santa Claus exists because we believe he exists but, more powerfully, because our father says so.

Armed with the untested depth of this inner knowledge, we face our life and pretend that our beliefs are solving our problems. We pretend that father knows best.

Mother, Do You Really Love Me?

Some of the teachers we meet are women. There aren't many. The spiritual game has been dominated by men for a long time. Despite our sophisticated political understanding and the correctness of the way we think and act in relation to women, for some of us, the female represents the love of our mother.

A few seekers may feel that they were born to mothers who couldn't properly express their love. These might have been mothers who gave up on natural birth and used painkillers, or used some iconoclastic delivery method that birthed their child in a large tub infused with warm chamomile while underwater speakers played meditative music. Or perhaps these were mothers who didn't breast-feed their child or enjoyed breast-feeding too much, who weaned the kids too early or too late, who criticized their child's pitiful attempts at individuation, or who smothered the child with unearned adulation, or who otherwise ruined their offspring.

Since childhood, some of us have never been too sure about our emotional world. Are we lovable or not? Does the world nourish us simply because we exist, or do we have to go through a tantrum to get what we need? Why do we have a deep aversion to chamomile tea?

Then we see the teacher. She is beautiful, beatific, and loving. She gazes at us with a look that says that the adulation is deserved, that our attempts at individuation are beyond criticism, that her nourishment is ours by right, and, above all, that we are special because we have her in our life. We have found our mother and she loves us more than anything. She loves us more than the other hundred people sitting in the meditation hall listening to her speak, this guru.

Those who listen are unaware of these, our deepest of fantasies. Each of the hundred is occupied. After all, they have each found their mom.

Perhaps it is time to step back, have a cup of chamomile tea, and get some perspective.

What Faust Learned the Hard Way

When we give up our own intelligence, our own perspective, our own direct contact with life, in exchange for the teachings of a spiritual authority, we expect something back. We are making a deal and we expect a good return. We want security, power, immortality, or maybe just a bit of respite from the nagging neurosis of our own mind. We can make that deal, but will we collect our end of the bargain?

At first it looks that way. We don't ask too many questions. We go along with the program. We smile a lot. Our new circumstance begins to look quite nice. We have friends. We have activities. We have a range of impressive insights into the worlds of spirit and matter.

We're happy. Well, not quite, but close enough. Well, actually, not very. We're getting by. The smile is cracking. Our friends in the group are wondering whether we are really wholehearted in our involvement and are starting to avoid us. We notice the human foibles of the teacher, the contradictions, the excuses. We try to forget what we see, but we can't.

Suddenly we are on the outside looking in. We are unbelievers. We asked too many questions. And we are alone. We are precisely where we were when we made our deal and, in fact, where we have been all along.

What Faust learned the hard way is that when you make a deal with the devil, you get what you want, but you also get what you don't want. In the world of deals, the one who wants something has already lost. The desire obscures our perception. The devil is dancing in delight. He has seen it before. Heaven may be hard to get into, but in hell there is always room for one more.

WHAT ARE WE AFRAID OF?

When our belief in authority is shattered, we are terrified. We are alone and unsure. We have failed as a disciple. Now nothing will prevent us from failing as an individual.

But what are we really afraid of?

Individuals cannot fail. Unless we reside within a belief system, we cannot find the criteria for failure. A life without authority puts us in direct contact with the effect of our life, our actions, our thoughts and feelings. Without the screen of belief we have direct perception of the world in which we exist.

Now we experience the actuality of anger, not the moral indignation of it. We experience the actuality of violence, not the theoretical condemnation of it. We don't act out of a historic or cultural ethical code but rather the actual experience of relationship with the world around us.

We don't act out of love because Jesus taught us to but rather because we have discovered love for ourselves. We don't act out of compassion because Buddha said so but because the deep experience of the pain of the human condition wells up in us.

We stand alone in the field of our thoughts, responsible for our actions, guided by no one and blaming no one. We are not guided by religion, we are living religion. We have become the prophet, the saint, the seer. In the moment that we relinquish all authority, all conditioning, all projections of memory, both inner and outer, we are an empty vessel that is filled spontaneously with life itself.

When the devil comes to make his deal with us, he can't find us anywhere. He looks and looks, but all he can find is life—vital, thriving, loving. He goes back to his realm, muttering profound curses. He relieves his disappointment by returning to his work with renewed vigor, only a small part of which is training those who aspire to be spiritual teachers. It is a small part of his work, but he enjoys it enormously.

THE RESPONSIBILITY OF THE INDIVIDUAL

Without a code of behavior, a system of belief, a moral teaching to follow, we are no longer constrained by anything. We have absolute freedom and, with that, a great deal of power. We act as individuals and as an expression of life itself.

This is the description of a mystic. It also describes the madman, the sociopath, the megalomaniac. How do we know we have not come to madness in the guise of understanding?

The madman lives in a self-created universe divided from life and out of communication with the world around him. He cannot maintain his universe if he is open to the whole.

We can only discover the actuality of our own state in communication with the world around us, in the openness that allows everything to touch us. This is a tremendous responsibility, but it is also effortless.

Walls that divide us from life take effort. Maintaining barriers requires energy. Openness is simple relaxation, letting go and giving up. The message of life will come through clearly in this state of openness.

ACTUALITY MEDITATION

WE ARE ALL MEDITATION MASTERS

We have tried all kinds of meditation techniques. We are still conflicted, neurotic, unfulfilled.

We sit down exhausted from our efforts, dispirited. We throw out the whole idea of meditating. We give up.

And there we are. We have finally come to where we are.

Where we are is meditation, wherever we are.

There is no entry and no exit. There is no doing and no not-doing. There is no technique, no result, no power, no experience.

The meditation of where we are is not even spiritual. It is life itself, moving of its own accord, fluid, quiet, beautiful, and self-fulfilled.

Where we are, there is no meditator, only meditation. There is no thinker, only thought. There is no doer, only action. There is no lover, only love.

We do not need a special time or place to be where we are. We do not need to retreat, to isolate, in order to be where we are. We do not need anything. We need nothing.

Nothing is what is necessary to be where we are.

We are all meditation masters. This is our birthright.

Most of us don't realize this. That is our curse.

Realize it.

Relax.

Recognize where you are.

WHAT IS ACTUALITY, ACTUALLY?

What is this actuality we have happened upon, not so much through our efforts but despite them?

We have not been able to discover actuality with our highly trained minds. We have only found more mind interpreting mind, interpreting mind, ad infinitum. We have not been able to find actuality through our vast collection of spiritual practices. We have only found behavior and belief. We have been looking for actuality in all the wrong places.

Now we have happened upon it, here, just now.

Is actuality so simple and so available? If we stop trying, stop doing, stop pushing and shoving our experiences around while trying to make them into something, does actuality unfold before us in the simple act of being?

Actuality. It is one more word. Now take away the word and what is left?

Actuality is the remainder, the bare, fundamental, uninterpreted quality that we naturally apprehend when the interpreter, the "me" is silent. Actuality is thought without identification of a thinker. It is pleasure and pain, as the feelings occur, without the distortion of our desperate urgency to find one and avoid the other.

But even the urgency, the distortion, the avoidance is actuality because this is part of our world and can only be understood if it, too, is seen without comment or conceptualization. Actuality includes the conceptual world, which acts to distort, as much as it includes the silence, which clarifies what is distorted.

Actuality is not simply the phenomenon that occurs but it is the very nature of the observer of this phenomenon. In actuality, there is no observer. In actuality, there is only the phenomenon.

To find actuality, try to find the self, the "me" who is commenting and interpreting. Of course, this "me" cannot be found, because the "me" does not exist—in actuality.

In the astonishment of not finding this "me" anywhere, we may stumble upon actuality.

Time—It Keeps Everything from Happening All at Once

Eternity's a terrible thought. I mean, where's it all going to end?

—*Tom Stoppard,* Rosencratz and Guildenstern Are Dead

One of the great contexts in which we all live is time. It is time that gives us the sense of past and future and that constantly impels us out of the timeless present. It is time that keeps us reflecting on our history and projecting our future based on that history.

If we are to discover the actuality of our life, we must understand the nature of time. We often think of it as a given, an assumption of fact that is reinforced by the obvious cyclical movements of nature, the historical cross-referencing of our memories with the memories of others, and the highly accurate predictive properties that we associate with time.

Does time exist outside of the web of conceptualization? Let us explore the question as if we didn't know the answer already. Let us look from the timeless state of the moment rather than the time-bound state of thought. Perhaps then we can understand the actuality of time.

In the timeless view of the moment, time looks like thought; the thought of now, the thought of then, the thought of will be. These thoughts arise and pass away in the eternal present. In this present, we cannot find the past or the future, other than the thought-of-past or the thought-of-future.

―――――――

EXPERIMENT: Check your clock and note the time. Now, sit with your eyes closed so you can closely attend to your conceptual world. See if you can find past or future. See if you can find thoughts-of-past or thoughts-of-future. Can you find any thought that lasts longer than the present moment? When you become too restless to continue attentively, stop and note the time on the clock.

―――――――

Time has passed, no doubt. Did you observe its passing while attending to your ideation? Or do we extrapolate time from the movement of the clock?

The close attention to our thoughts, feelings, and sensations—

our window on the world—seems to take us out of time. Yet the movement of the clock hands, the rising and setting of the sun, the aging of our bodies tell us that some progressive movement or series of changes is occurring.

Thought has noticed this, too. Its function is to predict the movements of the world around us and to protect ourselves and all that we consider to be ours. This is a decisive advantage in the survival game, and we not only survived but we dominated and destroyed anything that stood in our way—through thought.

Thought, being the memory and predictive function of our human system, did not invent time. Nor did it merely observe time, as in the natural cycles of the world. Thought, the memory of history and the prediction of the future, *is* time.

Without thought organizing the changing world into the sequence we think of as time, everything would happen all at once. Without time there would only be the present moment for anything and everything to occur.

From the vantage of timelessness, this appears to be simply the way it is. But from the vantage of time, timelessness looks like some sort of mental illness or, perhaps, enlightenment, depending on the cultural context. Time can only approach timelessness by buffering itself with highly theoretical mathematics, physics, existential philosophy, or religiomystical mythology.

In our culture, the only people who get to talk much about timelessness are the time priests: the science-fiction writers; a handful of celebrity physicists; and a few heavily marketed pop New Age authors selling repackaged Eastern philosophy. We let them talk about it, because that is what they are supposed to do. We listen, in awe and confusion, because that is what we are supposed to do.

But *we* can't talk about timelessness, or we'll end up at the county facility on a seventy-two-hour hold. Normal people don't discuss such things in polite company, certainly not at work and definitely not in front of the kids. After all, obviously time exists. It's how we know when to go to work, what day of the month to pay the bills, and what year we will start collecting Social Security. Time gives order to the movement of our lives.

Or does it?

We will have to deal with time if we are interested in understanding our lives. We may have to explore it, experience it, even talk about it. Even in our busy life, we'll have to find . . . the time.

PSYCHOLOGICAL TIME

Time is an amazing occurrence, unprecedented in the evolution of life on this planet. The arising of thought/time gave us both our salvation and our destruction. With the tasting of this particular fruit, we stepped out of the garden of prethought timelessness. Falling from grace, we began the incredible technological relationship to the natural world that we still have today.

As we developed the intricacies of the manipulation of the natural world through time/thought, through science, mathematics, language, politics, and war sciences, we easily forgot the timeless quality of the natural world. Our sense of time, with its foundation in the observed cycles of the world, expanded to include psychological time.

Technology relies on concrete time, the memory and prediction of natural phenomena. Concrete time references objective reality, like the rising of the sun or the decaying of atomic material. Psychological time relies on nothing more than its sense of separation, identity, and selfhood. Psychological time has only subjective reality to refer to, and its core reality is our sense of "me." Much as the arising of thought created concrete time, the arising of the sense of selfhood, of separation of "me" and "you" as discrete and divided entities, created psychological time.

Somewhere in our human history, the collective became the individual. The individuation of thought and the beginning of a concept of "me" brought about psychological time. This conceptual wrong turn gifted us with the disconnected world we now inhabit.

Psychological time is disembodied from the natural world. It exists only in the conceptual world. The emergence of psychological time changed our technological relationship to the natural world to an aberration. From hunter-gatherers, we became destroyer-hoarders.

Today time is not measured solely by a clock or the seasons of the year. It is also measured by the urgencies of achievement or failure, adolescent angst, the midlife crisis, the loneliness of old age. We are benchmarked against other members of generation X, the baby boomers, the Pepsi generation, or some other demographic nightmare creation. Merchants of consumerism stimulate us to go somewhere, get something, or do something—call now, don't miss this chance, today only. We experience constant time pressure, to get somewhere, do something, become something. We are told not to waste time, that time is money.

We have accepted our inherited outlook on time, a perspective that tells us we are separate beings, working with limited amounts of time to negotiate our success or failure relative to the success and failure of others.

In our psychological time frame, there are situations where there is "too much time," such as when we are bored, unhappy, lonely, anticipating, or in pain. There are situations when there is "too little time," such as when we are having exciting or stimulating experiences, when we are happy or experiencing pleasure, or when we feel the urgency of having many things to do.

When we are influenced by concrete time, as thought, we seek to prevent physical pain and ensure physical survival. But when we are driven by psychological time/thought, we try to prevent conceptual pain and to ensure conceptual pleasure.

Psychological time is the relationship of aversion and attraction to certain experiences. We want more mental pleasure and less mental pain, so pleasure is never enough (time) and pain is always too much (time). Psychological time merges pleasure and pain into a continuum of underlying discomfort and obscures the actuality of the moment. Psychological time drives us to sort our experiences frantically in an attempt to gain control over our life. We try to ensure that the conceptual center, the "me," never experiences psychological pain. This drive is pointless simply because the actuality of life is not in our control despite our efforts to rein it in; indeed, psychological pain is created entirely by the drive to prevent psychological pain.

Our search for the end of pain is useless because the source of the pain is that which is searching. The dividing of the world into a "me" and "you," the very isolation of separation, is inherently painful. The "me" rants and raves, churning out thought after thought, trying in an ever more panicked manner to find the end of psychological pain. We try therapy, drugs, religion, spirituality, meditation, but nothing seems to work.

It can't work, because the doer, the one who wants to get better, is the problem. The "me" is the pain. The end of pain can come only when the "me," the separation, the isolation, comes to an end.

Psychological pain can only come to an end when the resistance to the movement of life comes to an end. Now the bare actuality can emerge, freed from our futile sorting of psychological experiences into good and bad, painful and pleasurable, like and dislike.

Until then, we run like gerbils in our caged exercise wheel, running away from and toward the very creation of our minds—psychological time. No matter what we do, however much energy we expend, we always end up at the same point. We find pleasure. It turns to discomfort. We run from the discomfort to a new pleasure. That pleasure turns to discomfort. Soon, even the idea of losing the pleasure becomes painful. We run faster. There isn't much time.

Can we see the pattern, the endless cycle of psychological thought/time? Can we stand absolutely still on the wheel and stop spinning? Can psychological time, the endless becoming, the drive to pleasure that becomes pain, come to a still point?

This stillness is not devoid of endless neurotic thoughts. It is simply unmoved by them. This is a simple but fundamentally radical relationship to the thoughts, feelings, and sensations that typically drive our actions.

We are not trying to rid ourselves of anything. We are not trying to create a blank state. The quiet that we have come to is a nonreactive state. It is not particularly interested in evaluating what is arising in our field of awareness.

Now we are simply being. The world of thought, the world of reality, is in motion. The world of concrete time, the organization of change by thought, is still in motion. But we are not in motion, because in the discovery of stillness we also discover the end of psychological time.

This still point resides in each of us and is accessible in any moment, without mediation or help. It occurs spontaneously when we see the repetitive cycle of craving and aversion generated through the illusion of psychological time and when we know that we have gone around the wheel enough.

This point of recognition is a doorway to actuality, through which we have already stepped.

What happens now is our first full contact with the bare fact of our life, the discovery of what it is to be a human . . . being.

Other Extremely Heavy Considerations on the Nature of Mind and Reality

The nature of thought is such that it creates a thinker. This is a very odd phenomenon, but it is the very core of our personal conflict and the fragmented social structures that have grown out of our existential confusion.

The thinker doesn't create the thought. Thought creates the thinker. Each thought or feeling that occurs to us brings with it the idea of self, of a central, integrated entity that is generating the thoughts and feelings. But is this center actual? Is there a self, a "me," and, if so, where can it be found?

We quickly answer that this "me" is our body, or our brain, or our mind, or our soul. But let us investigate this question carefully and thoroughly before we answer.

———————

EXPERIMENT: Sit comfortably in any way you like. Bring your attention to your thoughts (concepts, emotions, sensations, and so forth). Look very carefully at the point of occurrence, that is, where the thought begins and also to the point of decay, where the thought ends. Where does a thought come from and where does it go? Is there anything that is stimulating, generating, or constructing a thought? Is there anything that directly connects one thought to the next (other than a new thought that has as its content the concept of connection)?

———————

EXPERIMENT: Sit comfortably in any way you like. Bring your attention to your thoughts. Can you observe what it is that gives you the sense of ownership of the thoughts that occur? What makes a thought, feeling, or sensation "me"? Is this sense of "me-ness" a thought form, an aspect of each thought as it occurs, or something else altogether?

What if our existence is simply the arising of thought in a field of awareness? Thought's nature is to divide the world, and this division creates at least the appearance of a subject ("me")–object ("you") world. In consideration of itself, thought again divides into subject and object, thinker and thought.

Thought thinks this way.

That is its inherent nature.

Thought can't think in any other structure.

What if the idea of a core entity doing the thinking is just that—another idea? Does life look a little different from this perspective?

It looks a little different to quantum physicists, who will tell us that the idea of finding the location of anything is futile, let alone this evanescent "me." In the quantum physical world, location is a bit suspect anyway since particles once having interacted with each other will always affect each other regardless of how far apart they are. They are essentially inseparable, although separated in space, and their connectivity is apparently faster than the known physical universe should allow. This seems to imply a connection that is beyond time and space, a connection that makes what appears to be two into something that cannot clearly be divided into two.

These physicists, the modern-day wizards, find that the very act of measurement, of looking at the location of a particle, changes the particle. They point to a universe that is not made up of particles with separate points of location acting on one another but a kind of cosmic soup where particles are energetically inseparable and whose location and behavior exist only in probability.

Given the apparent chaos of the physical universe and the difficulty of finding out where anything is or even separating it from anything else, it is no wonder we invented ourselves and have clung unrelentingly to the idea of "me" ever since. Otherwise we'd never get to the office on time, let alone get anything done.

Out of this unindividuated soup, sometime near the dawning of the human era and out of the preintellectual actuality of the natural world, we became self-aware.

This was not a moment of discovery. It was a moment of invention.

Thought organized the soup into parts. Thought invented the thinker and, since thinkers have to be somewhere, the place that the thinker resided became the body.

The body is not the mind, the mind is not the body, thought asserted.

Thought, since it could not think in undivided terms, thought in terms of a mind/body dichotomy. As this concept developed through history, through the accumulation and embellishment of thought organizing change as time, we developed paradigms that expressed this divided outlook.

Medicine ended up treating symptoms, diseases, and injuries, as well as "mental" illnesses. These were found in the body or the mind. Only on the fringes lingered the notion that there was no discrete body, separated from mind, separated from family, separated from society, separated from the natural world.

The invention of the body allowed for complex theological, philosophical, and religious practices to develop. We were no longer living life, now we were encapsulated in a body trying to find our way back to Eden. We had our drives and pleasures to overcome, our austerities to perform. With the invention of the body, we had created much more than a home for the thinker because we also concomitantly invented the spirit or soul. You can't have a body without having a not-body, the opposite, the ethereal aspect of what once was whole.

With the creation of the body/spirit, dualism was truly born. Before this we had the instinctual relationship to the natural world, the appetites and reactions that life brings into anything that lives. But once we had a dual world, a world of "me" and "you," of body and mind, of body and spirit, of spirit and mind, we had a rapidly dividing zygote soon to be born as the complex reality in which we exist today.

This reality, this world of concept, is a world devoid of contact with anything actual and everything symbolic. We generate this world with our thoughts, and we contact it in our thoughts. We have forgotten that there is anything else. We have forgotten individually and we have forgotten culturally.

But simply because we inhabit this conceptual world and have forgotten that anything else ever existed does not mean that there is nothing else.

Whatever is not this conceptual world, this vivid dream of thought's telling, is still there, waiting, silent and still.

Because this silence is not captured by thought, it is not divided. Because it is not divided, it is inclusive of thought. It is not thought, yet it includes thought.

We'll have to think about that one for a while.

EXPERIMENT: Use your thinking function to analyze the following statements. Pay careful attention to the states of mind/feelings that occur as you grapple with these koan-like lines that are synthesized from classic mystics:

Silence includes thought but is not thought.

That which is looking is what it is looking for.

The thinker is the thought.

If you find the answer, it is not the answer.

Does your mind tend to run from the contemplation or thinking of these statements? What happens to thought when faced with paradox, contradiction, or nonlinear consideration? If your mind is able to grapple with these statements, what is occurring in the space around the thinking while the mind is busy?

The recognition of the limitation of thought, its divided nature and the entangled, conceptual fabric of our everyday reality, is itself a koan.

What is the silence that includes all of this ideation but is not it?

This question does not occur in order to be answered with one more concept.

This question is the sound of one thought thinking . . . without a thinker.

The sound of one thought thinking is actuality.

The sound of one thought thinking is meditation.

This is actuality meditation. We are thinking without subscription to the belief in a thinker. We are feeling without the belief in a "me" who is doing the feeling. We are doing without the indoctrination of a doer. We are living in full contact with the bare actuality of life. We are living without the unconscious assumption of a discrete self that resides in our body, animates our mind, and searches for our spirit.

ENLIGHTEN UP — BEYOND MEDITATION INTO . . . LIFE. YIKES!

The idea of enlightenment is one of the greatest burdens and most daunting obstacles in our spiritual life.

As it turns out, it is impossible to achieve.

We can't get there.

Nothing gets to this heaven of realization by passing through the particular needle of enlightenment—rich people, poor people, camels, it's all the same. Enlightenment requires total extinction of the self. This is the same self that is trying to get enlightenment. Ipso facto big problema.

We can deal with this in a few different ways.

We can surrender and trust in grace—a plea bargain that we hope works out. But we're not too sure it will.

We can put in our cushion time, meditating, "practicing" the way an enlightened mind is supposed to be and giving ourselves the span of, say, a hundred thousand lifetimes to get it right. This is a considerable time commitment, and with our busy lives, who can really afford to block out a hundred lifetimes, let alone a hundred thousand?

We can sign up with a charismatic teacher who will presumably impart this enlightenment thing to us through his or her presence, touch, glance, or—yes, this really happens—by drinking the guru's post-scrub-down bathwater.

Presuming we leave the bathwater to the rest of the devotees, does this sort of magical thinking really cut it in this postmodern age? It might also be noted that charismatic teachers usually take all your money because you won't need it since you are going to get enlightened, but they need it even though they are presumably already enlightened.

Make sense? It doesn't have to. Enlightenment is nonrational, isn't it?

We can simply act enlightened as much as possible and let it be known we probably are, in fact, enlightened, but are too humble to claim it. This requires being really cool in tense situations, accumulating a flowing, pastel wardrobe with no mustard stains, and being clever enough to say only profound, or at least enigmatic, things. This approach is difficult to maintain, so let's leave it to the performance artists. There are some truly great acts out there already.

We can become enlightenment anti-Christs, start smoking, wear black, get lots of tattoos and piercings, and just be so damn cynical about everything that nobody will care whether we are enlightened or not. We won't care either. Problem solved.

But why does this problem even exist? Who sold us on the idea of enlightenment? And why did we buy it?

Enlightenment is a classic, powerful meme.

Memes are those pesky, self-replicating, concept packages that zoologist Richard Dawkins described in *The Selfish Gene*. When we discuss memes we are considering the contagious quality that allows thought to copy over from brain to brain in an ever-expanding way. Some thought bundles copy better and faster than others. Memes are a way of thinking about thought much as a geneticist thinks about genes.

If memes don't spread from brain to brain, they die out. The virulent thought chain letters that are memes demand adherence and replication. Their only purpose is to move up in the survival-of-the-fittest world of thought.

Meme theory, an admittedly grim perspective on our life, is itself not doing that well in the Darwinian struggle to find host brains. It is not spreading rapidly by finding new adherents. Memetics is being considered by only a few scattered academics and intellectuals. There are simply too many memes and not enough hosts.

In contrast, meme theory would suggest that religion, the king of meme categories, is swallowing up whole populations that are reproducing rapidly, creating new adherents. The great religions have all the components that compel reproduction of their particular beliefs. Encouraging high birth rates, rewarding proselytizing and punishing deviation from belief, reinforcing the accepted beliefs in the children and shunning those who stray—these are just some of the attributes of successful religious memes. Some religions thrive, some don't make it. Meme theory explains why Mormonism ranks as the fastest-growing religion in the United States (lots of children, everyone's a missionary, and don't ever try to leave the faith) and the Shakers are pretty much a history footnote (no sex, no children, no missionaries, great furniture).

This brings us to the idea of enlightenment. This particular meme is a bit of an underachiever in the religious meme category. It doesn't have the immediacy of the Messiah Coming or the zeal of being Born Again. It is certainly no match for a motivator like a good Holy War. Enlightenment is never going to be a top contender in the meme competition.

Enlightenment's hook is simple and it goes something like this: *You are in conflict and you know it. There is a state of mind in which you will not have to be in this conflict. This state is enlightenment and it could theoretically happen in the very next moment. But it probably won't happen in the next moment because you are just loaded with messy thoughts and habits and it's going to take an awfully long time to unwind all this mental junk. Probably lifetimes. Did we mention lifetimes, reincarnation, and all of that? That's why you have so much junk. You've been accumulating this for . . . well, pretty much forever. It'll take you about that long to fix it. But in the end, presuming you follow these practices during this somewhat lengthy period, you'll, without doubt—and doubt is one of those obscurations we'll have to get rid of—be enlightened. Enlightened, by the way, means that you won't have to struggle to be anything other*

than who you are and even the idea of getting enlightened will fall
away. It will be really cool and worth all the struggling, meditating,
and all of that. In the meantime, have a nice lifetime.

The strength of enlightenment is also its weakness. We all
know we are in conflict in our relationships, our work, our sense
of self, our fear of our own death, or just the day-to-day grind of
living. That's a big plus for the reproduction of the enlightenment meme. The enlightenment meme says we are in conflict but
suggests that there is a way out of the conflict and tells us how to
find the way out. The reward is the end of conflict: peace, satori,
cosmic consciousness, enlightenment. That's good stuff. It should
spread like a wildfire.

But here's the problem. The way out is *not* to try to get out of
the conflict. Trying is the very nature of our conflict, and here we
are trying to get free of trying. All we are left with is to stand still
in relationship to the movement of mind.

If we buy into the enlightenment meme, we buy into effort,
movement, getting somewhere different than where we are. But
if we are interested in enlightenment itself, then we are done. We
are who we are, where we are, without trying to make it different. The enlightenment meme dies with us. There is nothing to
reproduce, because there is nothing to do.

We got the chain letter, but we broke the chain.

Enlightenment is an idea, a myth that entrances us with the
story of getting somewhere other than the actuality of where we
are. This concept of enlightenment, which we have come to accept without question, is our irritating life companion, our greatest critic, and it constantly undermines our capacity simply to be.

How can we just be, when we should be better?

If we want enlightenment, then let's not wait a hundred thousand lifetimes for it. Have it now, by eradicating every trace of the enlightenment meme from our being. And, if we insist on a hundred thousand lifetimes, can we be honest and admit we have other agendas? We'll get to enlightenment when we are done with what we are actually doing with our first 99,999 lifetimes.

St. Augustine was straightforward in his prayer to God for enlightenment: "Give me chastity and self-restraint, but don't give it to me yet." St. Augustine was being honest. That's why he was a saint. Most of us are not saints.

Enlightenment is our excuse to live in time, to live from thought, and to navigate our life from a self-centered perspective. Enlightenment will always be out there in time, never here, never now. This is convenient.

If there is no enlightenment, then all we have is the actuality of our life. This is not convenient.

If there is no enlightenment, then we are brought crashing full force in collision with . . . ourselves.

If enlightenment exists it is something really special that only one in a zillion people ever achieves. For us it is going to take a long time. In fact, none of us will ever be enlightened within the scale of knowable time, and we will live out our life pretty much as we like with the simple excuse that enlightenment is not in this lifetime.

But if there is no enlightenment, then we are all fully responsible now.

We have two competing submemes: enlightenment now with immediate and complete responsibility or enlightenment later with the same responsibility, but fortunately much later. There is Now or Later.

A future enlightenment will rapidly win the Darwinian war for memetic dominance. The mind loves procrastination.

But here's the rub. The movement of thought takes place in a field of awareness, and the observation of this movement transforms it.

Our awareness of these opposite concepts of enlightenment changes them. We have made a deal with the future enlightenment to have a few thousand lifetimes of indulgence, but once we are aware of our irresponsibility, our deal doesn't work as well.

Indulgence requires unconsciousness.

The pursuit of enlightenment requires unconsciousness.

We are now aware of all of this. We are no longer unconscious.

But still this new understanding isn't sufficient.

Our vantage point even distorts the ideal of being present and responsible as the expression of enlightenment. After all, if we are present and responsible, there seem to be a lot of others who are caught up in irresponsibility and time.

We are not them.

We are better, in the moment, responsible, separate—and stuck.

The light of awareness shines on our convoluted mess of pretentious presentness. We can see it for what it is—the kind of addiction to perfection that only a sophisticated spiritual seeker could create.

We thought if we were present and responsible we would be perfect.

We thought that if we were perfect, we would be enlightened.

We thought if we were enlightened, we would be safe.

Now we see that we are not perfect nor are we enlightened. Awareness, the field of consciousness in which all of our thought structures arise and decay, shatters the world of competing concepts and spiritual stances. It shatters enlightenment itself.

Awareness is a slap hard across the face of the hysterical, self-obsessed, micromanaging spiritual seeker. Awareness says: *Snap out of it. You won't find life in meditation no matter how spiritually perfect-serious you become. Meditation is actuality, it is life itself, just as it is. Enlighten up.*

We have dropped into an unmediated contact with the structures of our mind. There is no enlightenment. There is no unconsciousness. There is no judgment of good or bad, right or wrong.

There is just what is.

And what is, is us.

THE NONPRACTICE OF
ACTUALITY MEDITATION

When we find ourselves simply with ourselves, stripped of our most cherished ideas of spirituality, and stripped, even, of a solid sense of self, we are in direct contact with life.

This contact is the only meditation that is free of a goal, free of a promise, free of our self.

Before this, we meditated in order to get better, to change, to perform, to escape. Now we meditate because that is all there is. It is entirely choiceless and motiveless.

We used to sit to meditate, at a particular time and doing a particular practice. Now we are meditating wherever we are, whatever we are doing.

Actuality meditation is not a practice.

There is no rehearsal for life. Practice doesn't make perfect.

Actuality meditation is a nonpractice.

It is the play itself, unrehearsed, unprepared, raw, fresh, and vital.

Nonpractice makes imperfect, and imperfect is perfectly fine.

It is the way we are, in actuality.

We are singing opera in the shower where no critics care to listen and artistic greatness visits all of us through the stream of rushing water. Then we remember who we are, how late we are for our appointment, and that we really can't sing. We have begun practicing our life again, and our nonpractice of actuality meditation fades into doing.

Yet even this intrusion of thought is actuality—the pressure of judgment, the rush of time, the insistence of neurotic thought, is the nature of our reality now.

Without effort or action, we find ourselves meditating on this actuality. Actuality meditation has become the fact, as it is, whatever it is, the awakening to the dream within the dream.

The dream goes on, but we are fully awake to it.

BREATH AND BODY
IN ACTUALITY

Space is almost infinite. As a matter of fact, we think it is.

—Dan Quayle

THE NAKED SINGULARITY
AND ALMOST INFINITE SPACE

Once we explore the nature of our minds through meditation, we inevitably come in contact with the mysterious world of our body. We know a great deal about our body, and, we soon discover, we know very little about it. We are motivated by the body's drives and desires. We identify closely with its pains and pleasures. If there is anything in the world that we know beyond a shadow of doubt is our identity, our very being, it is our bodies.

But are we our bodies?

Biology says we are the body. Religion says we are not. Science and philosophy have danced with each other on this issue over the centuries, sometimes agreeing, more often disagreeing. Contemporary science (e.g., quantum physics) is moving away from the purely material viewpoint, while philosophy (e.g., secular humanism) is moving toward it. Pseudoscience (e.g., some forms of psychology) wants it both ways, by dealing with our mind, which is deemed material (by locating it in the brain) and nonmaterial (by identifying its so-called afflictions in behavior, in neurosis, in ego conflicts, and so forth).

We want so badly for the world to make sense. It would be very nice if the world was created by a Big Bang so long ago that there is time enough in the immensity of history for simple randomness to create the complex and interrelated life form that we now have. In that case, our bodies would be the result of the natural selection process and the apex of evolution. But can we really believe the tale? Isn't something besides the massive explosion of matter at work here?

The physicists and astronomers can't exactly agree. Only a handful of people can even check their work. Their work consists primarily of mathematical calculations, and since many of us cannot balance our checkbooks with any degree of accuracy, we are intuitively concerned about explanations based on arithmetic. We know that there are three groups of people in the world, those who can count and those of us who can't. We are a little suspicious of the group that can use numbers well, or at least the group that can use numbers so well we have no idea what they are doing.

The other problem we have with the scientific paradigm is that the story changes every few years. Recently one of the handful of those who can, actually did check Stephen Hawking's work on naked singularities, a kind of black hole. Hawking was wrong. The story made the news. We all had a laugh. *A Brief History of Time* still sits on our shelf, waiting for us to finish reading it. And life moves on.

We define naked singularities as similar to black holes. Black holes we define as regions of space that are isolated from the rest of the universe because nothing can escape the gravitational pull of the infinite mass inside them. We talk about black holes as if we've seen them—well, not exactly seen them since even light can't escape their irresistible pull—but at least we counted that infinite mass inside to make sure it is really infinite and not just a whole heck of a lot. Well, okay, we don't know much about this stuff, but we have Hawking's book and even though we didn't read it, we read the reviews.

Then we see that funny story about Hawking being wrong and congratulating the guy who proved that he was wrong by giving him a T-shirt. Hawking says okay, maybe a naked singularity is possible, but really, really unlikely. The guy had proven with some fancy computer work that a black hole could collapse into a single point where space is infinitely curved and where, by the way, the laws of physics collapse, as well. Whoops. So much for physics. It collapses along with everything into a single point. The single point is infinitely curved. It's kind of like a black hole. We're following this, we think.

The T-shirt Hawking gives to the guy who proved him wrong says, "Nature abhors a naked singularity." We get a good laugh out of this. A naked singularity is like a black hole, so we suppose this is all funny.

Later we start getting an odd feeling. If Hawking is wrong about this, what else is he wrong about, and who is going to check him? Who is going to check the guy who found out Hawking was wrong? How come they get to change their story so often and people still take them seriously? A single point where space is infinitely curved? It's in the newspapers, it's in *Time* magazine. If we believe this, we can believe anything.

Why not believe in God? God created the universe in all its complexity. God created Stephen Hawking and the guy who proved him wrong. If there is naked singularity, God created that, too. God even gets on the cover of *Time* magazine from time to time. There's no way to check the math here, either. We could believe this. It is as plausible as quantum physics.

We could believe that Atlantis sank in the ocean thousands of years ago. We could believe that an archangel is being channeled or the ascended masters are speaking through any number of otherwise undistinguished individuals. We can believe in just about anything, once we get going.

If we are going to explore the nature of the body we cannot get caught in the battle of ideas, the dialectic of materialism versus the spiritual, or of any of the innumerable beliefs we have inherited as part of our culture or personal upbringing. This is easy to say, but difficult to do.

What Is Our Body, Anyway?

Our exploration of the body is largely the discovery and investigation of our ideas about our body. Without these ideas obscuring our view, perhaps we can see what our bodies are in actuality. We all started out without our body. Somewhere along the line we acquired one. That's quite interesting, if we really consider it.

We begin to develop as part of our mother's body, and only with a great deal of time and biological effort do we individuate. We are thrown out of the womb and suddenly we have a body of our own. Before leaving the body of our mother, we had shared so much with her that neither of us was sure where to find the dividing line. Now it is clear.

We are cold, hungry, and tired. We scream. Warmth comes, the breast comes, sleep comes. We awaken. We are wet, hungry, and tired. Dry diapers come, the breast comes, sleep comes.

The body is our only contact with the world. Our body is the world. Not a bad life, really, and we are certainly getting plenty of rest.

But this story develops a more complex plot.

Soon we are experiencing the urges of exploration. Our hand moves. How did that happen? It moves again. This time we moved it. Soon we can move it anytime we want. Eventually we learn to wave with it. The body has emerged as our expression to the world, not just our contact point with the world. The body is no longer the world, but our place in the world. The body has become the fulcrum upon which the lever of our mind begins to move the universe around us.

This division of outer and inner worlds mediated by the body, the interior world of thought and the external material world, is reinforced by the emergence of language. Language provides a means to categorize, manipulate, and control the world around us by the expression of the interior world of our thoughts. In the early part of our life, language explodes in our consciousness and with it our reality is altered forever.

We learn "no" and "don't." We discover "I want" and "mine." We have been expelled from Eden. We have become entombed in language, innocence swallowed in millennia of conditioning, both biological and cultural. After all, every word has a history. No word is pure. We take on the contaminants as we take on the words.

As our world becomes more and more entrenched in language, several things happen. We forget the prelinguistic state, which was not divided by thought. We become submerged in a language-based reality with all its inherent conditioning, and this reality becomes our only reality.

And, as our world becomes verbalized, we lose the primal contact with our body.

EXPERIMENT: Sit with your body. Take some time in a quiet place, without any distractions and without any particular idea of what you are doing, and just be. Pay attention to what you can find in your body and what part your mind plays in generating ideas about the body. What is the actuality of the experience with the body?

EXPERIMENT: Sit with your eyes closed, and move your attention through your body beginning at the top of your head and going slowly back and forth across the field of sensation that you know as your body—to the outer body boundaries and back again. When you become aware of anything in this interior world, attend to it until it changes or dissipates. Move through the whole body, or any part of it, until your concentration drops. What is body and what is mind in this world? What is the actuality of what you discover?

———————————

EXPERIMENT: Lie flat on a comfortable mat. Relax. What are the barriers to full relaxation? What are the physical or mental tensions? Where are they? Are they in your body or your mind? Where is your body or your mind? Are they the same or different? If you fall asleep during this rigorous investigation, you can consider that one of the more pleasant side effects of the life of exploration. Enjoy your nap. By the way, what is sleep?

———————————

THE BODY AS A TOXIC WASTE DUMP

Physical concepts are the free creations of the human mind and are not, however it may seem, uniquely determined by the external world.

—Albert Einstein

The complexity of our thought structure buffers us from the direct sensory contact with the world. We can barely discern the actuality of our bodily impressions amidst our mental commentary. We feel all the pleasures and pains, except that they are now interpreted by our burgeoning intellect, our ever-expanding collection of thoughts, ideas, and words.

We make an appointment to visit a dentist about a painful tooth. There is pain, but, let us say, there is also a great dislike of going to a dentist.

Pain in the tooth has been supplemented with fear and aversion.

"I don't want to go to the dentist" and "I hate dentists."

We can add a layer or two of anxiety to that.

"I couldn't sleep last night thinking about the dentist appointment."

Add a portion of guilt.

"I shouldn't feel so anxious, it isn't normal."

Add some tension, a sedative, and some painkillers. The drill starts. Is there pain? No. Well, not exactly. There is a difference between suppressing the awareness of pain and no pain. The tooth is being drilled. We just don't feel it. The hole is there.

And the mind has stored the aversion, anxiety, and guilt as memory, as psychological pain. But we will simply forget that. We will cover it over.

We don't want to be in contact with our body at the dentist or any other time there is pain—any kind of pain—physical or psychological. This seems perfectly reasonable. Painlessness means happiness, doesn't it?

Not exactly.

When we deny the presence of conflict in our mental or psychological world, isn't the hole still there? The damage is done. The pain is stored, waiting patiently to be experienced. The storehouse is our body.

The body holds the experience and holds it tightly. The body, once fresh and supple, becomes gnarled with age and experience, unresponsive, unbending, unable to change and to learn.

Just like us.

That is to say, just like what we have come to identify with—our minds. Our bodies hold our pain, our memories hold the pain, but we, the ineffable self, don't have to experience the pain.

Of course, we are kidding ourselves. We don't escape the pain. It comes in the form of disease, unhappiness, boredom, failed relationships, and a thousand other forms. It comes in the low-grade gnawing of a life without deep contact with the substance of our life and in the acute expression of the fear of death and disease. We can run, but we can't hide.

Pain is one of our companions in life and rather than experience it, we shove it deep into our bodies.

Like toxic waste, pain can be transported, encapsulated, buried, and forgotten, but eventually it will come bubbling to the surface of our life more poisonous than when we dumped it.

We have built labyrinthine mental constructs to avoid psychological pain. We hide within these conceptual creations, within our armored bodies. This constructed world, the avoidance, the hiding, the knotted body, becomes our only reality.

Fear of pain has become the pain, and this pain becomes our reality.

Fear and pain cannot conceive of anything else. Release from this state of contraction becomes a threat. We resist all attempts to liberate us from our world, because we have lost sight of any alternative.

At some earlier point in our life, we may have seen the pursuit of pleasure as the alternative. As actively as we avoided pain, we sought pleasure. Even as our body was storing the pain that we avoided, it was being taught the cravings of the addiction to pleasure.

The body can experience pleasure, but it cannot crave it, it cannot indulge in it, it cannot connive to increase it. The mind must do all of that. For the body, pleasure is the simple fact of a particular experience. For us, for the collection of concepts that we have organized as our "self," pleasure is much more.

For us, pleasure is the reason to be, the drive to become, the reward for our efforts, the solace after our failures. Pleasure is not in this moment. It is always in the next moment or the last moment. We train our bodies to remember and to anticipate. We amplify our memory into craving. The craving must be satisfied. We do what we have to do to satisfy our cravings. We indulge until we are sated. But the strange thing about pleasure is that we are never satisfied. We are often sated, but never satisfied.

The next morning, the next hour, the next moment, we want it again. We want more, better, stronger, higher, or more often. We want. The wanting is stored in the body. The body craves sugar, caffeine, nicotine, food, alcohol, cocaine, pot, sex, endorphins, and on and on. The wanting is never satisfied. The wanting is a constant irritant. There is no end. We can no longer remember a life without the wanting.

We fear that we won't get what we want. It is painful to experience our lack or even the possibility that we will lack what gives us pleasure. The search for pleasure is painful. We are gobbling the pleasure as fast as we can find it, hardly experiencing it, searching for more, panicking, desperate, and in pain.

Pleasure is pain.

The toxic waste is bubbling up.

EXPERIMENT: Try one day of responding directly to your body's signals. If the body is hungry, eat; thirsty, drink; tired, sleep; and so forth. We generally bring the body along for the ride our minds create. We feed our bodies fancy food designed to stimulate our taste buds whether we are hungry or not, we dose it with caffeine when we have to impress or perform, we push it past fatigue in order to get everything done in a day. What if we let the body run the show for a day? A week? A month?

EXPERIMENT: Try one day of letting the body respond directly to the mind's signals, without the control and limitation of the mind. When the mind feels fear, let the body run, rather than sit in tension. When the body is angry, let it scream and express, rather than store the anger in its guts. What are the boundaries past which we will not let the body go? Violence? Sexual advances? Socially unacceptable physical expressions? Notice what happens when we hit these boundaries. Where does the action that we make ourselves stop from happening go?

EXPERIMENT: Investigate your body ailments. Most of us have the beginning of disease formation, stresses, areas of pain or dysfunction in our bodies. What is the source of this in your body? Do you hold this illness or stress in a fixed way? Do you avoid it? Do you incorporate it in your sense of self? Would you miss it if it were gone?

———————

THE BODY AS A BELIEF SYSTEM

It's no wonder that with all of the stress and conflict going on in our poor bodies, we'd rather not consider the whole situation. So we don't.

Instead we just believe in what we have been told about our bodies. We have so much to believe in and so little reason to question anything. It is easier this way.

We learned at a very early age that bodies should be hidden because naked bodies are erotic bodies, although of course adults don't exactly say that. They don't say much of anything about bodies, and that communicates their whole perspective much better than words.

We also learn early on whether we are good or bad, thin or fat, cute or not. We learn how to dress and how to behave. Sit still, don't touch, that's dirty, be quiet. We learn about food. Finish the food on your plate, don't eat that, this is good for you, wait until dinner. We learn that a sick body gets attention or avoids punishment. Some of our bodies are good at sports and some aren't so good. Some are good at attracting a mate and some aren't so good.

We learn that the body is an object that should be beautiful but sometimes isn't. We learn that we smell, our hair is unkempt, our waists too plump, our breasts too small. Our pathetic skin is either too dry, too oily, or possibly both, and needs a tan if it is white and some miracle to whiten it if it is dark.

We may be lucky to be a cute child, but adolescence snatches us into awkwardness, from which we emerge for a moment of youthful beauty before plunging into the long, downhill sagging slide into middle-age frump and, finally, old-age bags and wrinkles.

Our physical drives and appetites are supposed to be restrained in our youth when we have the energy to actualize them. Yet we are required to flaunt these same drives as a measure of our self-worth when we are distracted and exhausted in our later years. Sex is demanded and feared, talked about and taboo, regulated, rationed, and measured throughout our life. So is food. So are drugs and alcohol.

At least we can have all the caffeine we want.

THE CHAKRAS — ARE THEY THERE OR NOT?

One of the curiosities one encounters in the investigation of the body is the idea of chakras. This system of energy centers in the body has been around in our culture in a big way since Madame Blavatsky founded the Theosophical Society in 1875 and began propagating such notions. Much of the conceptual framework comes from Hinduism and various Yogic philosophies, and the real explosion in chakrology came in the sixties and seventies with the massive influx into Western culture of Eastern religion and meditation teachings.

The popular idea of chakras suggests that there are centers of energy that are not physical but are generally referenced as physical. There are a lot of variations, but most systems agree that there is a sexual center at the genitals, a solar plexus around the navel, a heart center, a throat center, and a third-eye center in the middle of the forehead. Some systems add another center of energy at the base of the spine and a wildly blissful, thousand-petaled-lotus light spectacular at or just above the top of the head.

Most people can easily get a sense of at least some of these chakras. Different qualities seem to occur when we focus our attention on various areas of our bodies. When we encounter an angry person and our stomach rolls we can certainly note that this is different from when we meet that nice person who warms our heart. In the hands of a good spiritual trainer, these common feelings can be formed into a system of "thinking about" these experiences that will soon have us discussing our chakras as if they were tangibly there.

We can meditate on the chakras. We can chant and visualize the chakras. We can read books about the chakras. We can learn about why people do or don't heal based on their chakras. We certainly know people who are stuck in one chakra or another—always angry, always sexual, or bug-eyed from too much of that third-eye stuff.

But are the chakras there or not?

Do we really encounter any experience that is in a location? Is there a heart chakra that vibrates in some kind of cosmic isolation from the rest of us?

Or do we need a story to explain the actuality of experience, a story that will bring cause and effect to a world that seems chaotic and acausal? Our direct experience anchors the chakra story, and yet it is embellished and spun into a tale that takes us away from this unmediated contact and transports us magically into the land of belief. Here we are protected from the chaos and given a very implausible, but nevertheless comforting, system of understanding our experiences.

Chakra stories are told to us by experts. These are people who have the surety of knowledge of how these energies work.

They teach us.

We learn.

They speak.

We listen.

And we pay them.

These energy experts have changed only a little over the years. Where once exotic swamis, yogis, and transcendentalists of the East held court, now slickly packaged medical intuitives, psychic psychiatrists, and healers of the New Age reign.

We are not taught *how* to experience but *what* to experience— and *where* to experience it. We have learned a new language, a new set of concepts, a new way to interpret.

Once again, we have disconnected from actuality.

EXPERIMENT: Let's find out about the chakras. Sit in a quiet place. Close your eyes and bring your attention to your breathing. After you have developed sufficient concentration from "watching" the breath going in and out, bring your attention to the bottom-most area in your body where you can find any quality of gathered or congealed energy.

Keep your attention there and note the qualities that seem to occur, both in pure sensation, feelings, or emotions, and thoughts, memories, or ideas.

Now, find the energetic center that is next "up" from the first one. Explore in the same way. Continue "up" the body. At some point, you will run out of body and you will be done exploring the chakras.

You may find three areas that seem to be collection areas, you may find seven, you may find none. You may note different general qualities in these areas. You may not. You may note a fluid feeling as your mind and what it is investigating moves from center to center, or you may experience what seems like the release of energy, muscle tension, mind tension, or memory. You may have deep feelings of terror or bliss. You may have the feeling of boredom, hurting knees, or the desire to get on with the rest of your day.

Can you can see the actuality of what is there? Is there anything there?

EXPERIMENT: Read any book on chakras. Sit, concentrate, and bring your attention to the areas described by the book. Do you see what is described in the book in this area of your body?

Try harder.

Now do you see it? Good. Isn't that really amazing?

———————

EXPERIMENT: Try investigating, rather than reacting to, the feelings that occur in the relationships in your life. You may often encounter people and experience their "energy." For example, you meet a person who is angry and you find your stomach tighten, or you talk to that lovely friend who makes your heart feel so expansive. When this occurs, notice where the experience seems to be located, where you are feeling it. Why is this particular experience happening in this context? When did the quality you are experiencing begin and when did it stop? Is it being transmitted by the person you encounter? Is the experience located in both of you? Is there only one thing happening, which is somehow shared by both of you? We often hold constructed stories of how we experience these qualities with each other and never investigate the actuality. We tend to explain what is happening in our field of experience in subject/object terms (e.g., I met Bob and he really made me angry). As an experiment, begin to investigate these encounters and shifts of feeling without the explanation you usually carry with you.

———————

EXPERIMENT: Sit and explore the energy centers of your body. It doesn't make any difference whether you are discovering what is there directly, or through a description found in a book or through a teacher. When you find a body center, pay attention to its qualities. Now can you find where the viewer of these qualities is located? Who is exploring the centers and where is the viewer positioned— inside the energy center, outside the energy center? If you find the viewer/viewpoint, pay attention to this viewpoint. What are its qualities? Now where is the viewer who is attending to this viewpoint? Continue this exploration until you have discovered the context that is observing the chakras, the context that is observing anything and everything. See if you can find yourself, the observer, located anywhere.

If the chakras aren't the observer and the observer can't be located anywhere, then what are the chakras? Whose are they? Do they exist?

THE BODY AS ACTUALITY

Every world picture is and always remains a construct of mind and cannot be proved to have any other existence.

—Erwin Schrödinger

The actuality of the body is that it isn't.

Our cultural viewpoint is so obsessed with the either/or thinking process that it demands a body and a mind. There is no such thing. The body and mind do not exist in separation but are inextricably one, not just with each other but with everything.

We can experience our body conceptually, as biology, as physiology, as self. We can experience it sensorially as hot, cold, pain, pleasure. We can experience it energetically as vital, fatigued, dense, spacious. There are many ways that we can experience the body.

But we can never experience the body in actuality.

There is no body to contact, just as there is nobody to make the contact.

In actuality, when the mind/body dichotomy collapses there is only one thing happening, and that one thing is neither subject nor object. The actuality is without the thought that divides the world and without the world that embodies the thought. The actuality is unified.

This quantum body, the nondual confluence of all that is in each moment is the base reality in which our life takes place. It is not separate from anything, except in the individuation that conceptual thought brings with it.

This conceptual framework, with which we navigate the totality, is the creator of the body and is the origin of the body's disease, aging, and, ultimately, death. Thought creates the body and the mind. Thought creates the friction of separation. Thought is at the root of disease and death.

Without the separation of thought, without the creation of "me" and "my body," is there disease or death? Who is sick? Who dies?

What occurs if thought does not hold us hostage to its ideas of duality and life moves through us without hindrance?

Let us breathe.

Let life breathe us, and find out.

LEARNING HOW TO BREATHE—
AREN'T WE BREATHING ALREADY?

An interesting correlation exists between our breath and our state of consciousness. This becomes evident whenever we sit and pay attention to the breath.

Simply attending to the breath brings about an immediate relaxation response. The body tends to release its tension and, with that, the breath deepens. Some meditation techniques teach attention by way of the breath, directing students to notice the slight sensation created by the breath at the tip of the nostrils.

This practice has the effect of concentrating the mind and cultivating a sense of awareness. It also becomes obvious after a short time of "watching" the breath that our minds incessantly seek distraction. Over and over again the mind will skip from the breath to thoughts, fantasies, memories. Over and over again we can bring our attention back to the sensation of breath.

After some time of this, most people feel more focused, attentive, and relaxed. It is a simple way to experiment with your own mind/body process. It is not difficult and not dangerous.

There are dozens of systems of teaching about breathing. These systems purport to do everything from releasing childhood trauma to bringing on cosmic consciousness.

There appears to be a relationship between breath and

thought. But there is also a relationship between thought and breath.

Training ourselves to breathe differently changes the way we think. But at the same time, we are also retraining the way we think, and this new thinking changes the way we breathe. Have we freed ourselves, or have we taken on some new conditioning?

We have not discovered what we are, yet we are ready to change ourselves into something better. We will learn to breathe better so that we will be better. Do we need to learn how to breathe, or is the breathing that we are already doing the very expression of what we are?

Do we need to retrain ourselves—and what is it that we are training to be? If we are to discover the actuality, then isn't our breathing, just as it is, the actuality we seek? Do we need to learn to breathe, or are we already breathing?

What is the breath? What is actually occurring when we breathe? What is breathing when we breathe without an attempt to modify, restrict, enhance, or even understand what is occurring? This exploration cannot be systematized or taught. It comes out the intensity of the individual to inquire into the nature of life.

The very first thing we do in life is to breathe. Nobody told us how or why. Since then, we have been conditioned in every imaginable way to have a secondhand experience of our life.

We have even been told how to breathe.

We don't need to learn how to breathe.

We are already breathing.

Breathe.

THE EXPLORATION OF BREATH
AND STATES OF MIND

Without the burden of the ideas of the body, mind, and breath we can begin to explore the actuality of our experience.

———————————

EXPERIMENT: Breathe. Attend just to breathing. What qualities occur at the point of intake and the point of expulsion of breath? How do these qualities affect the breathing itself? Does this change with attention?

———————————

EXPERIMENT: Breathe. Attend just to breathing. Pause at the point of intake and the point of expulsion. What happens during these pauses; what are the qualities that occur when breath is suspended?

———————————

EXPERIMENT: Breathe more rapidly and attend to the qualities that arise when the breath rate is accelerated. Notice feelings, thoughts, images that may be occurring. You may find that evoking these same aspects of your mind will tend to increase your breathing rate. For example, if you imagine a terrifying monster, you will tend to breathe faster.

Try breathing more slowly than normal. Again, notice the aspects of your mind that arise when your breathing is slowed down. Try evoking the feelings, thoughts, images that occur when the breath slows down, and see if this slows your breathing rate.

———————————

EXPERIMENT: As you move through your day, notice the relationship between your breath and the states of mind that you experience. Does the mind create breath, or does breath create the mind? Is breath breathing thought, or is thought thinking breath? Are the mind and the breath one thing or two things?

———————————

EXPERIMENT: Breathe. Now attend to the breath. Now find the point of observation of the breath. Is awareness inside or outside the breath? What is the context in which breath is taking place?

ACTUALITY MEDITATION
WITHOUT REALLY TRYING

*For a man who has let himself be drawn completely out
of himself by his activity, nothing is more difficult than to
sit still and rest, doing nothing at all. The very act of rest-
ing is the hardest and most courageous act he can perform: and often it is quite beyond his power.*

*We must first recover the possession of our being be-
fore we can act wisely or taste any experience in its human reality. As long as we are not in our possession, all
our activity is futile.*

—Thomas Merton, *No Man Is an Island*

DOING NOTHING IS HARD TO DO

In any moment of being, without psychological doing, without
grasping for anything in particular, we experience a profound
connection to life around us.

This is the connection that we say we want.

But we can't seem to stop doing long enough to do nothing.
We feel compelled to be doing something all the time.

Why is it that doing nothing is so hard to do? Even when we
set out to do nothing, we do nothing with great intention, with
vigor and dedicated seriousness. We work hard, we play hard,
and, spiritually, we "do nothing" hard.

We're that kind of people. If we weren't the hard-driving

folks we apparently are, we might never have emerged from the evolutionary fracas as Homo supremo. We wouldn't have conquered—cut down, killed, burned, dug up, or paved over—the natural world. As a civilization we would never have created the Age of Reason, the Renaissance, or the Space Age, or, for that matter, the Dark Age, the Inquisition, or the New Age. We wouldn't have invented things like adjustable-rate mortgages, armor-piercing bullets, repressed memories, and call waiting. If we weren't as aggressive as we are, some other species would be, and the world would be run by fire ants or hyenas.

We do it because somebody has to, and frankly, we do it best.

The dominant cultural paradigm arising out of all of this un-fettered aggression is, of course, the American culture. The American culture is not really just about democracy, or free enterprise, or liberty. It is, not surprisingly, the Top Dog Aggression Culture and its message is Consume or Be Consumed. We have trounced just about any country we've tangled with, and where we couldn't beat them we invested heavily in them or loaned them into International Monetary Fund mortgage oblivion. We sold them Pepsi and Big Macs, CNN and MTV, Madonna and Michael. They never knew what hit them. We're that good.

Our message is simple and it sells: Just Do It. Do what? It. Just do it.

Just do it. Do. Do.

This is the mantra of the Age of Consumption. Do it. Don't wait. Don't miss out. Don't be dull. Don't be uncool. Don't be poor. Don't be confused. Don't feel. Don't be. Do. Do. Do it.

We believe. We're Doing It.

Then one day we hear something radically disturbing, something about being, not doing.

We hear in the cacophony of cultural sound bites, news segments, and commercials a slight gap in the continuity of action. This is the sound track from the nightmare of every hot media producer.

What we hear is dead space.

We hear what we are never supposed to hear. We hear nothing.

We hear the absence of the hype, the information overload, the demand to consume. The cultural context drops away for a moment, and for a moment we are absolutely still. This is radical. And, better, it's free.

Now the noise starts again, but this time we hear the gap of silence after each sound bite. We are hearing a different message. Just be.

Just be. Be. Be.

Just do it. Just be. Do. Be. Do. Be.

Either Frank Sinatra is on the radio or there is something very interesting going on. We thought doing nothing was hard to do, but we have discovered that "doing" is porous and "being" infiltrates through the holes.

Our conditioning is to act, our nature is to be. Our history is doing, our present is doing nothing. Our culture says consume, our relatedness says share.

Doing nothing isn't hard to do.

Just be it.

EXPERIMENT: Media Meditation—Examine your own cultural context like an anthropologist from the planet Zygon.

Watch television, listen to the radio, read the newspaper without getting drawn into either the content or the medium itself.

Since these media are vehicles for entertainment and information and are designed to distract, the first meditation is to pay attention to the form without concern for the content.

Can you follow the camera changing every five seconds on television, the way the eyes skip around on a newspaper page absorbing tragic headlines and grocery coupons with the same glance, the hypnotic drone of radio? What is the effect of these various forms on you? What qualities are created in your mind and body in response to the medium itself?

Now observe the content, regardless of the form of delivery. Note the urgency of everything from a catastrophic news event to a three-day automobile close-out sale. Is anything good happening anywhere, or is there only death, tragedy, and destruction . . . and a whole lot of sex? Do you notice any urges occurring, like a sudden desire to order a pizza or run to the Gap for a quick shopping blitz?

Turn off the sound and watch the television without

the audio. Is the nature of the medium clearer when there is only one thing happening?

Now turn off the sound and the picture. Is the nature of the medium clearer when there is nothing happening?

Looking for a Solution Is the Problem

When it comes right down to it, our problem is that we are looking for a solution to our problem.

We know we have a problem.

We're dissatisfied with our lives.

We look for a solution. We are told there is one.

The solutions don't work. The meditations, the drugs, the spiritual trips, the religions. Nada.

That is because the problem isn't the dissatisfaction.

The dissatisfaction is a symptom.

The problem is the seeker. The problem is the "me" looking to feel good, to gain control, to find relief from the fear that it—the "me"—doesn't exist.

The fear is a symptom.

The fact is that the "me" can't get better, because the "me" doesn't exist.

The "me" doesn't exist outside its own construction. The "me" doesn't exist outside its own dissatisfaction, its own fear, its own search for a solution to the "me."

Looking for a solution is the problem, because the "me" that is looking is the problem.

This problem doesn't exist.

We all know we have this problem.

This problem doesn't exist.

The End of the Spiritual Seeker

If there is no problem, then what are we searching for? If there is no problem other than the construction of a "me" by thought, a "me" that has no inherent existence outside of this mental world, then why do we search?

Has searching become a habit, an addiction that fills our psychic space with a sense of purpose and meaning? Can the constant pushing past the obvious, the concrete, the actuality, into the projection of hope bring us anything other than more of the same pushing?

Spirituality is a social construction, an agreement to see the world in a particular way and to behave in a certain way. The spiritual searcher is the cornerstone of this construction. Without the search, spirituality fades into the absolute stillness of actuality. Without the searcher, there is no search, there is no spirituality, there is no center, there is simply the movement of life. This is what the spiritual search is supposed to be searching for, and yet the search, the searcher is all that is in the way.

This thin veil of illusion is maintained by the effort to pierce it.

In actuality there is no spirituality.

Six Experiments in Meditation

1. Go into a room and don't come out for one day. Don't do anything in that room.

2. Pay attention to your thoughts for a few moments. Don't think about bright red roses.

3. Pay attention to your thoughts for a few moments. Don't think about anything.

4. Sense your body, starting with your toes and working your way through the entirety of your body. Do you experience from a particular location in your body? Where is the location from which you are experiencing? Locate and experience that place. From what point are you feeling that place? Locate and feel that place. Keep going. Where does consciousness reside? Is there a location from which we experience and, if not, what is it that is experiencing?

5. For twenty-four hours be completely honest with everyone regardless of consequences.

6. Reflect on your own death. If you were to die at the end of the day, how would your day be spent? The end of the hour? The end of this moment?

Spreading the Silence —
The Dialogue Experiment

What happens in a room full of people who have come to the end of the spiritual searching, who have deconstructed the consensus reality of religious beliefs and have discarded hierarchical structures?

This experiment is going on right now in many parts of the world in the form of dialogue designed to find out if individuals can sit together in a nonauthoritative way and inquire into the nature of our mind and consciousness. Dialogue is at the cutting edge of a new human paradigm.

David Bohm, a renowned physicist, began experimenting with dialogue groups after years of interacting with J. Krishnamurti in the form of one-on-one dialogues. The Bohm dialogue groups attempted to bring people together, not out of a common belief system but out of a common need to understand the nature of belief and the nature of dialogue itself.

A dialogue group is formed to explore within itself, without a particular agenda or format, but with the intention to look deeply at the conceptual mind and the silence out of which it arises. Because these groups are generally unstructured, the group itself will discover the inherent pressures to create leadership and the tendencies to accept certain beliefs generated within the dialogue itself. The vitality of the dialogue comes from the intensity of each person and his need to set aside his ideas and to engage in the discovery of something entirely new. Some elements of dialogue are predictable, some are surprising.

Groups tend to degenerate and lose direction without a focusing agent. This is why spiritual teachers are the norm in groups. Often participants are impatient with this tendency and fail to allow the chaos to self-discover itself. We are conditioned from an early age to expect hierarchically based group processes, which are orderly and efficient. Disorder has always been considered bad, punished and eliminated.

In dialogue we are concerned with actuality, not with process or conclusions. We discover that there are no apparent rules. This in its own right is a shock to our system. Chaos may result from the absence of rules.

We try applying our ideas and philosophies to the chaos. But these are transparent because the dialogue group is intently interested in actuality and keenly aware of concept acting as if it were actual. Are there rules that do not come from belief? If not, then the idea we try to introduce will not find a foothold in the dialogue.

Sometimes there is a takeover of the dialogue by forceful individuals; whether they are deeply insightful or totally fragmented doesn't matter. A leader, as is shown by history, needs only to lead, and followers gather no matter how destructive or how clear the leader. In dialogue, these takeovers are short-lived, because they are also transparent.

Many times a group comes together to explore dialogue and ends up as a debating society or a philosophers club. We hardly know what else to do with ourselves other then expound on our collected theories of life. We are profoundly identified with our ideas about life and yet the dialogue is the discovery of what is left when these ideas are deconstructed. We become the Explorers Club as we enter into unknown territory.

Often a dialogue group will be unable to find its own meaning or purpose. It will self-doubt. It will decay into a state of collective ennui. Finding nothing, we may abandon the dialogue and return to a debate. We are relieved to find meaning, at last. We feel better already. We take comfort in repeating old ideas we dredge up and feel the solidity that comes with expounding the known. We have forgotten that a dialogue is the exploration of the unknown and the expression of nothingness.

Sometimes a dialogue group will discover a profound silence, where there is no evidence of separation, no need for explanation. Sometimes there is a crackling, focused energy of discovery. Sometimes there is the sense of liberation brought about by confusion. Sometimes there is the laughter that accompanies the acting out of a divine comedy.

A dialogue group will often be focused by an individual. This will look much like the authority figure of a teacher. This structure can be addressed directly so as to make it clear—this is what I am doing, there is no implicit authority in this doing—and this structure can change at any time. The nature of dialogue is such that it is inherently vigilant to the constant attempts at creating power-based relationships, projections, and reactions in relation to the position created by the individual who is focusing the group.

While a dialogue group may be attentive to the creation of power, a powerful individual can be attentive to any imposed restrictions on his or her own expression, even when it is dominating in nature. This restriction may arise from an idea of egalitarianism.

The whole group interaction is out in the open so it can be examined. The actuality reveals itself.

Dialogue seems to have the possibility of embodying our collective intelligence and expressing the unindividuated quality of life. It is also an experiment that has the possibility of failing miserably because it cannot break free of the conditioned need for the certainty of belief and authority.

For those who enter into this exploration, the measure of its quality lies in the capacity to stay persistently engaged with the other participants in the dialogue, and focused on the actuality of what is occurring. Perhaps in that contact, with great humility and attention on the part of each person, that which separates will drop away and something new can emerge.

EXPERIMENT: Set up a dialogue group in your area. There is no process and there are no particular rules. The intention is the discovery of the actuality of who we are, not limited to our beliefs and philosophies. The group will inquire into the structures of thought, the nature of awareness, the forms of communication that make up the human being. Topics will occur spontaneously, as will silence. Everything is to be looked at. Stay engaged with each other and hold on to your hat.

EXPERIMENT: Take the group on spiritual field trips. Attend religious and spiritual functions, talks and teachings by spiritual luminaries, and try out the practices that are being taught. What is the actuality of these situations and the experiences that are generated there? Invite itinerant teachers and their entourage to attend a evening of dialogue in which their teaching is explored. Keep the apparent walls of the dialogue group porous so that life infiltrates and the dialogue group doesn't sink into its own form of separation and insularity. Inquire into topics like social action, politics, education, and psychology.

EXPERIMENT: If the dialogue group is able to stay engaged (many do not and quickly disintegrate), what is there to do together as an extension of the dialogue? Is there any collective action that arises? Does the mutual inquiry foster an intentional community or cooperative businesses? Does it suggest social action or charitable activity? Are their other forms of dialogue or communication?

EXPERIMENT: When a dialogue group stays engaged, can a deeper, nonverbal exploration take place? What happens when an engaged group comes to the end of words? What is the nature of group meditation in this silence?

Exploring the Silence —
Group Actuality Meditation

Head and heart are not apart
Sit-in in-vites you
Into new experiencing
As new all through
Doing (no thing) well

—Paul Reps, *What It Is Like*

One of the best ways to explore actuality is, not surprisingly, silently. This exploration can take place individually but also has an expression in a group.

Group meditations hold the potential for a great depth and also untold foolishness. We easily succumb to group psychology, in which we collectively agree to have certain meditation experiences, and then we have them. But what if we enter into such meditations without any agreements at all? What happens then?

Group meditation, like dialogue groups, offers a full range of possible experiences from the silly to the sublime. But, like dialogue groups, the exploration is the very group dynamic that is often a great trickster. What is the actuality of the meditative experience with a group of people? Is it the same as sitting alone, and, if not, then what is different? Are the qualities that occur in meditation in some way shared? What can be discovered about our collective meditative experience without mutual agreement or belief?

Unformatted meditation requires a tremendous passion on the part of the participant. There is nothing that explains why we are doing it. There is no obvious benefit. There is no system being practiced. There is simply what is.

Again, we crave a leader to show us the way. We want a systematic approach to the apparent chaos of our thoughts, emotions, and sensations. We want confirmation of our experiences and insights.

This can be found in a hundred different meditation systems, but it cannot be found here. Here, all we have is actuality—with each other.

If we can stay engaged, we may discover a completely different dimension of group dynamics. We are once again exploring the unknown.

Sitting together can only occur when there are not two, or three, or many. Sitting together occurs when there is nobody sitting. If there is somebody sitting, as it often appears there is, the meditation is not with others, it is with our self. What is this self? Why does it want others?

It is a great challenge to sit together and not ritualize it. Sitting doesn't require anything else. There is nothing to learn. There is no context that is better. There is no posture, mantra, breathing, or visualization that needs to be learned.

As ritual develops in a group, make it obvious and explore what it is.

Explore posture, mantra, breathing, and visualization.

Explore it all.

Sitting doesn't require any of it.

Sitting doesn't require exploration.

Sitting doesn't even require us.

EXPERIMENT: Sit in silence together with others who have a deep interest in the investigation of actuality. When the group loses its focus, stop. This stopping point is usually obvious (and often accompanied by much rustling, coughing, and clearing of throats). There can be dialogue about what has occurred, or not.

While sitting, notice the movement of mind to relate to the group setting, how we look for context for our experiences in the group experience. Notice the body tensions in relation to others present. As the sitting deepens, notice the changing qualities, both in what appears to be the personal mind and what appears to be the collective field of the group. Notice the deepening itself. Where does this come from? As it dissipates, where does it go? What is it that is aware of all of this? Is it the same or different for each participant?

PART THREE

WALKING-AROUND MEDITATION AND EVERYDAY LIFE

OUR THOUGHTS SEEM TO HAVE A MIND OF THEIR OWN

I have the impression that events take place in me, that in me things and passions rage and conflict; that I watch myself and see the fight of these hostile forces and that first one, and then the other, has the upper hand; a fight, a mental battleground and that the real me is this "I" who watches the "me" of events and conflicts. I am not these passions, it seems, I am he who sees, watches, comments, considers. I am also he who, ardently, wants another me.

—Eugene Ionesco, *Fragments of a Journal*

FRUSTRATED WITH OUR ANGER

Anger is a short madness.

—Virgil

There is one thing that can get even the most spiritual of us really hostile. Despite years of meditation, breath work, therapy, and visualization, there is one thing that we just can't stand, and we can't seem to do anything about it, either.

It really gets us riled up and ready to scream. Secretly, we'd like to kill this thing once and for all and get it out of our face.

This one thing is our anger.

Anger has us by our proverbial garbanzos. We think we're cool, but we're not. When anger arrives, we were cool, but now we're hot.

We try to control it, shape it, reduce it, and understand it, but anger gets the best of us every time.

We suppress it—it burns a hole in our stomach, raises our blood pressure, destroys our heart.

We express it—it embarrasses us, destroys our relationships, ruins our self-esteem.

We take it to the therapist. We trace its history through family and experience. We scream into pillows. But when we leave the therapist, anger goes home with us. We're distraught, confused, and . . . angry.

We take it to meditation class. We watch it. Anger arising, anger passing away. The guy in the next row is moving a lot and sniffling. He shouldn't come to meditation with a cold. We never liked him with his aloof attitude, like he knows better, when, in fact, he's totally inconsiderate. He deserves all the resentment we can dish on him. Now, where were we? Anger arising, anger passing away.

Our mate doesn't love us enough. Our boss doesn't pay us enough. Society doesn't recognize our talents. No wonder we're angry.

But mostly we're angry because we can't do anything about our anger. It keeps coming and there is nothing we can do.

There is nothing we can do.

There is nothing we can do. This is the fact. This is also our liberation.

There is nothing that anger hates worse than no response. It can feel its power draining out in the face of this nonresponse. It's got to get a response—reaction, guilt, shame—something. It will die if it is not fed.

What if anger started a war and nobody came? What if we become pacifists? Gandhi drove the British out of India by not fighting them. What would become of anger if we did absolutely nothing?

Q: Don't I want to do something to end this conflict?

A: Who's the doer? You suggest that you should do something. You have this entrenched psychological condition, whatever it is. You're angry at your husband all the time because he doesn't do the dishes. You come up with a program of what to do. You count to ten before you get angry. You say your mantra. You meditate fifteen minutes in the morning. You sit down with your husband and talk about childhood experiences. These are all "doing" things.

But who is the doer? What is the entity that is trying to correct its behavior? Where does that action actually come from? Isn't the action coming from the same bundle of memories that is the problem? The problem isn't to find a course of action. The problem is to understand the nature of the doer.

Q: So a solution can't be reached by doing something, it's just perpetuating more of the same, perhaps in a different form?

A: The action of doing is a movement out of the actuality. It's projecting a future where things will be better and it's coming up with a mental plan to get from where I am to where I want to be. That's not what life actually is. Life doesn't follow a plan of where I am and where I want to be. Life is what it is. The movement to change into what I want to be is the movement away from the actuality and because of this we never experience where we are. We can't even understand the nature of the problem. We're too busy mentally projecting where we want to be.

Q: Referring to the example about the husband never doing the dishes, so I'm angry: What is the dynamic in that of doing nothing?

A: What if you don't take any action whatsoever?

Q: Then I'll end up doing the dishes all of the time.

A: No, that's an action. I am now presently in my kitchen. I'm seething with anger. There's no action. What happens? If there's no action, there's only anger. There's no husband, no object of the anger. There is no causality, no rationale that because he didn't do the dishes therefore I'm angry. There's no doer. There's no holder of the anger—that is, the "me" isn't there. There's only anger.

What is possible now is understanding the nature of anger. The nature of anger is not causal. It's not because of my husband. It doesn't originate in me because there's no "me." It's not from my childhood. It's not from experience. Anger simply exists in nothing, out of nothing, as energy.

Q: But it's still painful to the experiencer. . . .

A: You'd have to find that out. The reaction to the anger is indeed mentalized as pain. But find that out for yourself directly, by taking no action, no remediation of that direct experience of anger, and see what its quality is. Is it painful? If anger doesn't have a creator or a recipient, it has a different quality.

Of course, you have to be willing not to get the dishes done. Most of us are so wrapped up in being productive. You have to be willing to stop, not get the dishes done, not get anything done, and maybe end up sitting on the kitchen floor with your anger.

Few people want to do that. So they blame it on their spouse or their parents. They blame it on an unhappy childhood or their stressful day at work.

EXPERIMENT: Next time you are angry, don't get involved in the object of the anger (who or what you are angry with), don't even get involved in the anger (the should, shouldn't, shouldn't be shouldn'ting, etc.). Instead, see if you can find the "me" who is angry. Who is doing the anger?

EXPERIMENT: Next time you are angry, pay attention to the physical attributes of anger. What happens to your breathing? What happens to your heart rate? What happens to your stomach? What happens to your posture and muscles? Who is doing all of this? Can you change any of these physical responses? If these conditions change, can you maintain your anger? Is there a psychological component to the physical, a physical component to the psychological, or is there only one thing happening?

Are We Afraid of a Life Without Fear?

Where a man will find no answer, he will find fear.

—Norman Cousins

The sun . . .
In dim eclipse, disastrous twilight sheds
On half the nations, and with fear of change
Perplexes monarchs.

—John Milton

We are driven by fear in our life because we are driven by the
need to assess and predict our environment, and to survive based
on that knowledge. Our biology recognizes its own survival strategy as a primary function and constantly alerts us to potential
danger. We use the tool most suited to this assessment, which is
our brain.

When we find danger, we analyze it and confront it, or avoid
it, based on which strategy is likely to succeed. We fight or run.

Biology in the human being has mutated through thought
into psychology. Now we are convinced through the urgency of
our own conceptual framework that we must assess the psychological dangers in our world. We must decide to fight or run, to
dominate or submit, based on our psychological survival.

Fear has become the moderator of our psychological well-
being. Despite the fact that this aspect of our experience is entirely conceptual, it has become so intertwined with our biology,
our conditioning, our reality, that it exists as if it were actual.

We are afraid of being hurt when we approach new relationships, as if we might be physically struck. What if they don't like us? We become shy or overly aggressive as we attempt to assess the qualities of a new environment. We are afraid.

Our heart pounds. The palms of our hands sweat. Our mouth is dry. Is there a predator stalking us in the jungle? No, we are being introduced to someone we don't know.

We are agitated. Adrenaline is rushing through our system. Our thoughts are racing. Are we in a fight to the death with another animal competing with us for food? No, we are giving a presentation to our boss on the new marketing plan.

Fear has left the jungle and entered the world of our mind. Virtually everything we do is filtered through psychological fear. We are motivated by fear. We are hindered by fear. We live in fear.

What should we do about this?

Let us recognize that, for the most part, fear is irrelevant.

Fear is functional for us when we cross the street and see a truck coming. Fear is useful when we are using power tools, driving a car, or otherwise putting our lives or our appendages on the line.

The rest of the time, fear is pointless. It exists as a protector of a psychological body and its appendages. This psychological body is not in need of protection. It is indestructible. You cannot hurt something that does not exist.

Fear makes the case that without its help, great damage will be done to us. Let us check the hypothesis. We'll keep the concrete fear—we'll watch out when we cross the street—but let us try living without psychological fear for a few days and see if we survive.

"No, no, no, can't be done, too dangerous, you could get hurt," says Fear.

"But I'd like to try it just for a few days," we say.

"Absolutely not. You'll be terrified. You'll be damaged. You don't have any idea what could happen without me!"

Fear is getting quite insistent. It has always protected us in the past. What would we do without this protector? After all, what would we be without fear?

What would we be if we were . . . fearless?

> *Since fear and love can hardly exist together, if we must*
> *choose between them, it is far safer to be feared than*
> *to be loved.*
>
> —Niccolò Machiavelli

> *There was a peace in their hearts. They were filled*
> *with the fearlessness of those who have lost everything,*
> *the fearlessness which is not easy to come by but*
> *which endures.*
>
> —Aleksandr Solzhenitsyn

Don't argue with fear. Fear always wins. Fear is always right. There are countless circumstances of which to be afraid. Fear has always protected us. Okay, maybe it is a bit smothering, but we're safe.

Fear can give us almost everything we need in life. Fear will make sure we are never touched by anything that will hurt us. We never know what could hurt us, so Fear will make sure we are never touched by anything. There is too much risk in being touched.

Fear does not like risk.

Fear can give us everything, except one thing—fear can never give us love.

Love waits for fear to fall silent. Fear knows nothing about love and cannot know that love is waiting. Love is the greatest gift Fear will ever receive.

Don't argue with fear.

Love fear.

Fear knows it has no actual existence and this terrifies it. Love fear for what it is—nothing avoiding itself, an illusion.

Fear is our psychological center looking for sustenance, for existence, for being.

Love has no center, has no fear, and exists only in pure being. It is a match made in heaven.

Love envelops fear.

ANXIETY AND STRESS: WORRY, BE UNHAPPY

When you get to a fork in the road, take it!

—Yogi Berra

We live in the age of anxiety.

We are overpopulated, overworked, overstimulated. We don't get enough sleep, enough relaxation, or enough time.

We are constantly receiving infothreats. Our population is mushrooming all over the world, and the whole world wants to move in next door. Terrorists are trying to blow up public buildings, planes, trains, whatever. Sexual predators stalk our children. Gunman kills seven and shoots self, film at five.

We are cajoled into working longer and harder by ever-increasing financial demands and doomsday predictions—social security won't survive the aging boomers, college costs increase faster than inflation, the gap between rich and poor widens, the crash of the monetary markets is coming. Preapproved credit card offers pour in with credit limits higher than the gross domestic product of some Third World countries. We consider them for a moment, these Gold Cards, or if we are quite special, Platinum Cards. We pretend we don't know that they are really just Plastic Cards and we sign up for a lifetime of spending.

It is time to get up, time to go to work, time to pick up the kids, time to go to meetings, events, plays, movies, shopping, return phone calls, more and more and more. And less and less time. More and more time pressure.

Less time, more to do, more to earn, more to spend, and we could die at any second from some irrational act of random violence or a new ultravirulent strain of disease exotica circulating through the climate control system at the mall.

What to do?

Be unhappy, worry.

What else can you do in the face of this depressing overload of bummed-out reality? We're stressed and we should be. Look at everything we go through in a day. We're anxious because we're perfectly normal. Anxiety is normal. It's the way we are, so why get stressed about it?

What is there to do about it anyway?

We think we know what to do about it, which is to think we know about it. We think that if we think more, collect ever-growing amounts of information and think about that, we will somehow survive. Without survival, what good would relaxing be, anyway?

Our brains are aflame with the search for more information about the things that stress us. If we find out more, we're less likely to be caught by surprise, we're more likely to know what to do. We'll know whether to fight or run.

We're not fighting and we're not running. We're collecting lots of information about the circumstance. We're thinking about fighting. We're thinking about running. But in actuality, we are sitting in our cars in rush-hour traffic, we're on the couch watching the news, we're sitting outside our supervisor's office waiting for a meeting.

Stress is the effect of mentally modeling the actions we might take or the actions we can't take and all the circumstances surrounding them, including most particularly our own injury, defeat, or destruction.

Stress is thinking.

Thinking thinks it is helping the problem, but helping the problem *is* the problem. Endlessly collecting the information that will solve the problem *is* the problem. Perpetually analyzing the information that will protect us *is* the problem.

We can't protect ourselves from life, we can only respond fully in the moment of challenge. Preparation to respond confuses the response. We are responding to what we prepared for, not to what is present. We are stressing ourselves for no reason at all.

In the moment of challenge, stress is the signal to act. The action occurs automatically, in response to the actuality of the situation.

In the anticipation of challenge, on the other hand, stress becomes the signal that we are thinking, modeling, analyzing the idea of a challenge, not the actuality. There is nothing to do in response to a conceptual challenge. No action arises automatically.

Conceptualizing crises and creating contingency plans is useful in the concrete world of building bridges, repairing heart valves, or waging wars. But in the psychological world, we model the survival of the "self" in relationship to conceptual challenges. Here, the deeper we go into contingency planning and survival strategies the more confused we become.

We can gather and analyze information until the end of time in a futile attempt to ensure the survival of this psychological center. We can impose higher and higher levels of stress on ourselves in an attempt to find protection.

We might as well give it up. We cannot protect a center that has no actuality.

Put down the alarming news article, turn off the shock television and combat-talk radio. There is no one to protect; there is no one to run; there is no one to be stressed.

EXPERIMENT: Try an infofast. We're not talking about carrot juice and colonic cleansing here.

This is worse.

No TV or newspaper, no books or magazines, no radio talk-show arguefests. For a week, turn it all off. Don't even indulge in long, gossipy conversations on the telephone or your computer chat rooms. Skip the reading, you'll have to put this book down for a while. Put away the novel you're halfway through.

Give it all a break.

Now watch your craving for information, calamity, and conflict become unbearably urgent. Don't confuse urgency with importance. Watch your mind cool down, the demand for stimulation subside.

What is happening to your anxiety level? Is the world still doomed? Does the world even exist?

If CNN covers the breaking news live and no one is there to watch, is it still news?

What is the nature of your life without infomania?

Now reintroduce one information source at a time. Read the newspaper the first day after your fast. Notice any reactions?

Add back another source each day until you have the whole crazed mess downloading into your frantic brain. Notice any difference in your feelings, thoughts, or need to consume products, services, beer, pizza?

Do you feel an increased sense of imminent death and destruction? Heightened anxiety? If the overload gets too overwhelming, you may want to check out that *60 Minutes* segment on depression, or tune in to that psychologist on the radio. Maybe more information will help.

———————————

Changing Our Mind on Drugs

We live in an interactive world. The reality of the world is not fixed nor is the mind that perceives it. There is constant dialogue between the apparent perceiver and the perceived. The substance and quality of what is apprehended changes the viewer, and the viewer changes what is seen.

This dialogue is reality. There are not two but one.

Traditional psychological models often posit a central and solid thing called mind, located in the brain, which is affected by elements it contacts.

From the standpoint of the mind, however, the psychological model is just one more experience.

The mind has a more fundamental dilemma.

It can't find itself.

Mind knows it isn't located in the brain, because sometimes it dreams of far-off places, moves with lightning speed to the mentalized past or future, and can feel itself to be in your foot or, even more confusing, in the very heart of a loved one.

The mind would like to find itself. It remembers in a vague, hazy sort of way that there was a time when it was everything. Maybe that was when the body was very young, or before the body was born, or in some other life, but the mind knows that there is more to mind than what the mind knows.

The mind is always looking for a way back, a way beyond, to a transcendental reality. It looks relentlessly for the soma, the magic mushroom, that will take it there. The mind will try everything and anything to find the right drug.

And it's all drugs.

Alcohol is drugs. Fast food is drugs. Violent movies are drugs. Shopping malls are drugs. Dollars are drugs. It's all drugs.

Everything the mind apprehends is a drug. Everything the mind touches transports it somewhere. Everything it ingests changes it. The mind cannot stop until it finds the transcendental, until it is taken beyond itself by the thing it contacts.

This basic drive to transcendental experience, experience beyond what we know, is the core of our spiritual search. The intuitive knowledge of our limitations compels us to seek what is outside our thought structures. Drugs have been used since the beginning of man in an attempt to experience that which is beyond the known.

For the spiritual searcher, pharmaceutical drugs present what appears to be a shortcut to transcendence. We take the drug. We have a wonderful or terrible experience. The drug wears off. We remember the experience, as if the remembering *is* the experience.

Of course, it is not.

The experience, whatever it was, is gone. The memory, the representation of the experience, is what we are left with.

We try again to capture the experience. We take the drug. We have the experience. The drug wears off. The memory remains, but it is not the actuality.

The problem with many drugs is not the drug experience. It is the attempt to capture the experience by memory, the distortion of the remembering mind, and the repetitive attempt to replicate the experience by taking more drugs.

Whether the experience is to get high, happy, or holy, the cycle is endless: the brain needs more and the mind remains the replicator of actuality, not the actuality itself.

On a societal level, the subject of drugs is so infused with controlling politics, mythology, pseudoscience, and cultural misinformation that we never seem to be able to clear away the obfuscations and actually explore the subject. Drugs present a number of difficulties. Some drugs lend themselves to addiction and consequent dependent or antisocial behavior. Some present apparently alternative realities creating apathy or disdain for the consensus realities. Some have effects that are confusing, hard to document, and difficult to explain. Then there are the drugs that are considered good, and are legal but regulated. Some legal drugs alter our minds and are controlled by specialized doctors. Our societies regulate and direct what the mind can experience because we fear that transcendental experience will destabilize our social structures and decentralize their power.

We have a War on some drugs, a Campaign to develop other drugs, and Programs to educate on still others. We don't know whether drug use is a crime, an illness, or a fact of life. Street drugs are bad. Psychiatric drugs are good. Medical drugs are good. Alcohol is bad and good.

Millions of children in the United States are given speed (usually Ritalin) by their schools (now they can pay attention in their drug-education classes), another half million or so receive antidepressants. Speed is given to kids who talk too much and who are overactive. Antidepressants are given to kids who don't talk enough and who are underactive. Meanwhile, researchers have noted that ritalin and cocaine have nearly identical effects on brain cells.

Kids too up, drug them down.

Kids too down, drug them up.

Kids just right, sell them beer and cigarettes.

In our confusion about drugs, are we raising generation Rx?

The U.S. Drug Enforcement Agency publishes brochures on how to keep kids off drugs. The U.S. Department of Education publishes brochures advising parents where they can get drug therapy for their kids.

We put poor kids who sell drugs in jail and celebrities in rehab. We plea-bargain the kingpins or take their company public, depending on the drug. We test employees for drug use, write prescriptions for drug use, search cars for drugs, advertise the latest drugs in full-page magazine spreads, and sponsor sporting events with drug—that is, alcohol—money.

We won't find much that is useful to our inquiry about drugs in our social agreements. Here we are too perplexed and afraid.

But this is not necessary. All experience could be unencumbered by fear. The thing the mind is looking for is not in experience. It is not in drugs. The revolution is elsewhere.

Experience can change the experiencer but can never take the experiencer, the mind, beyond itself. There is always the memory of the experience to hold the mind. Everything that brings experience is a drug in this fundamental respect.

What the mind is looking for is in nonexperience, is in silence, is in the collapse of the viewer and the viewed into the nonduality of being.

This is inherently free, legal, and unregulated.

Everything else is a drug.

The transformation of consciousness, not experience of any sort, is where the revolution is waiting.

Hurt, Failure, and Disappointment

We destroy our children at a young age. In a culture that values competition and dominance, we produce children without much consideration. Children are subjected to shame, control, physical punishment, and emotional isolation simply because their parents exist in the ignorance of their own conditioning. These parents were once children subjected to the same forces of shame, control, and violence.

We are these children. Many of us are also parents. But we have never gotten over our own childhood. We were born fresh, innocent, and wondering. We called for help, for love, for warmth. We cried for a response that couldn't come from our parents, because it had never come *to* our parents when they were children.

We were born with a trust in a life that had nurtured us in the warmth of the womb. But we soon lost that trust. We learned that we were wrong, failed, a disappointment. We learned to behave. We learned to respond in order to avoid punishment or to receive affection.

We grew up in environments of overt violence or covert neurosis. We limited our human potential to a set of behaviors that allowed us to survive, to compete, and to dominate or control.

We learned the human condition, an inheritance handed down from parent to child reaching back to the beginning of the human race.

Now we are adults. We live in this hurt, failure, and disappointment. We are driven by these feelings. If we achieve, it is never enough. We can never rest. We can never be. We are never just as we are, we are always becoming, striving to please, to succeed, to win the love and admiration of parents or parental symbols who are incapable of responding.

There is no way out. No amount of therapy or meditation will help. These attempts to change are simply more of the same—this is the failure looking for a new behavior that will please. If we can only find the inner child, recover our soul, or sit quietly watching our breath, then finally we will be whole and worthy and lovable.

There is no way out. This condition cannot be fixed. The very attempt to fix it, to be better, to please the imagined critic, is only aggravating the dilemma.

The child is the invention of the parent. The parent is the invention of the culture. The culture is the constructed reality of an endless chain of time and conditioning. Our hurt, our failure, our disappointment is an invention held in place by a host of inventions.

We were born free, as an expression of life itself. We are not a child of a parent of a culture. There is no actual demand on us to be any way at all. There is only invented demand. We do not need to find a created inner child nor do we need to resolve any issues with the symbols that are our parents. We do not need to succeed or be concerned with failure in a constructed culture.

We are the children of life, not the children of invention.

Life has only one demand of us, and it is inherently fulfilled by us.

Life demands of us that we be as we are.

That's it.

There is no failure.

Life is a wonderful parent. It infuses us with the totality of its parenthood both in demonstration and in communication of its qualities. It is the perfect parent because, without the demand of anything in return, it gives us freedom and responsibility.

We can never recover from being the children of our parents. That is because we are not the children of our parents, we are the children of Life.

In freedom there is no failure. In responsibility there is no hurt.

Life may appoint us the custodian and caregiver of a child. There is nothing more beautiful or challenging than when Life entrusts this task to us. But this is a function, not a position, not ownership, not a situation of power or control.

There are experts who will advise us on how to modify our children, how to make them stop crying, force them to feed on our schedule, make them sleep when we want them to sleep. These are experts in the destruction of the human spirit. They speak from the confusion they were raised in.

The expert on raising a child is the child.

A child is the gift of life to itself. A child is the expression of life and holds the intelligence that we have mostly forgotten. Only ignorance cannot see this in a child. And ignorance will try to make each child its own.

No one possesses a child.

A child is free.

In freedom there is no failure.

Be free, like a child.

FINDING SPACE — THE INNER FRONTIER

Our world is cluttered, overflowing, overloaded. How do we find space amidst all the clutter? How do we find a moment, an hour, a day that has a sense of openness, timelessness, spaciousness rather than the pressure of movement, achievement, survival, and not enough time? We can't even find the space in our life to do the yoga, meditation, tai chi, or whatever our spiritual practices that are supposed to create more space.

We're jammed.

Here's the trick. We don't find space. Space finds us.

We're lost in the woods. The worst thing to do is to wander around looking for the way out. Looking for a way out uses up our energy, makes us feel more and more frantic, and usually gets us even more confused and further from help.

The best thing to do when we are lost in the woods is to sit down, make a nice fire, and relax. The best thing is to wait for help to find us. If we're bored, we can make messages on the ground for airplanes to read.

We're lost in complexity. Looking for space in our life fills up the space of our life. It exhausts us and makes us feel more and more frantic and takes us further from help. Let the spaciousness of life find us.

It is always here, which is precisely where we are.

Relax. Help is very near.

Ever Stop to Think and
Forget to Start Again?

The spiritual seeker approached the great guru, and asked
him to describe the enlightened mind.
"My mind is perfectly empty," said the guru.
"I just can't believe that," said the seeker.
"Believe what?" said the guru.

In any moment that thought simply stops, we realize that we are part of the vast, unindividuated universe.

We realize this, and then we realize how profound it is.

We've started thinking again. We've returned rather quickly to an individuated world where thought is thinking, and the thinking is "me." This world of the "me" is not at all profound, and when we inhabit it, we long for the sublime world of no-thought, a world we think about a lot.

There is no real difficulty in accessing the world of silence. It is always there, in the space between thoughts. But this silence of self is broken by the insistence of thought, which tries to capture the silence and analyze it.

What if we stopped thinking, psychologically, and didn't start again? We would still have the full functioning of our perceptual fields. We would have access to memory as historical record. We would have knowledge of the technologies with which we are used to working. But we would not have the idea of a "me" who is doing any of this.

We would recognize that there is a biological body/mind plexus, but this aspect of unindividuated life, like the wave in the ocean or footprints in the sand, would be indistinguishable from the substance of what surrounds it.

It is only through the idea of a separate self that we can construct the reality we call "me." Without it, we are left only with life.

What would happen if this psychological thought went silent? Concrete thought, technological thought, perceptual and feeling thought would continue, but there would be no doer to be found.

EXPERIMENT: Watch the very next thought you have occur and decay into nothing. Where is the thinker in the moment this thought disappears, but before the next thought is generated? Now watch the next thought occur. Where did this thought come from and who is thinking it?

EXPERIMENT: When you open your eyes after meditating or being in deep relaxation for some time, or upon awaking from sleep, there are often a few moments where the perceptual field is active but the conceptual mind is not. What is happening in these moments where there is perception but no concept? How do you reconstruct your reality?

PART FOUR

GETTING

HERE

FROM

THERE

IN THE END
IT'S THE BEGINNING

FAITH WITHOUT BELIEF

Faith is the not-yet in the now: it is the taste of the fruit that does not yet exist.

—Laurens van der Post

So they stood on the shores of Faith and felt the old dog-mas and certainties ebbing away rapidly under their feet and between their toes, sapping the foundations upon which they stood, a sensation both agreeably stimulating and slightly unnerving. For we all like to believe, do we not, if only in stories?

—David Lodge

If we discard belief, aren't we left with a life devoid of context, meaning, and direction? How are we to live a life without belief? After all, belief gives us surety, and without this promise of certainty we are really only left with faith.

Faith is what is left when belief is burned in the fire of inquiry. Faith is belief gone through the Dark Night of the Soul.

Faith is not of the mind, it holds no promise from what is already known but rather what is not. In this freedom from the known, faith takes us into the vitality of each moment, fresh, new, and alive.

Belief is conditioned by thought. Faith is free of any ideation.

Belief is knowable. Faith is unknowable.

Belief separates. Faith includes.

Belief resists change. Faith is change.

Belief is the created. Faith is the creative.

Belief strives for Faith. Faith strives for nothing.

Belief is the Myth of Faith. Faith is the mystery of Life.

We cannot have Faith in Belief, nor can we Believe in Faith.

Belief is inherently insecure. Faith is unshakable.

Belief resists challenge. Faith has no challenge.

Belief looks for more believers. Faith waits silently.

Belief is anchored in the separation of our self in relationship to another. Faith is an expression of the whole to the whole, within the whole.

How do we live without belief? We live without the conflict of my ideas with your ideas. We live without the competition of self with other. We live without resistance to the movement of life.

We live in Faith. We live in the dynamic potential of existence, exploding in each moment, unpredictable, uncontrollable, and incredibly beautiful, and then fading into the profound silence of the universe. Faith is the recognition of the life force that animates this endless cycle of creation and decay.

We live in Faith because Faith lives in us, is us, and is all around us.

The End of Effort

*Consider the lilies of the field, how they grow; they toil
not, neither do they spin: and yet . . . even Solomon in all
his glory was not arrayed like one of these.*

—Jesus

Let us bring vitality into our life and our actuality meditation.
This is not effort. Effort requires a doer.

We are not going to get what we need by effort, we're going to
get what effort needs. Effort needs spiritual accomplishment,
recognition, and more stimulation to fuel more effort. We need
to come to the end of the pressure to get somewhere spiritually.

Save effort for the tennis match, walking the dog, practicing
the guitar. This is recreational effort.

Expend effort taking the kids to the zoo, mowing the lawn,
finishing the report. This is productive effort.

Spiritual effort doesn't work. There is really no such thing as
existential exertion. It's not worth the effort. There's no place to
push off from, anyway. And no place to get to.

Make an effort to not make an effort.

Try to relax. Try harder to relax. Try even harder.

Now make less effort to relax. Even less than that. Make absolutely no effort to relax.

We can't even accomplish the end of effort.

That's good news.

It means we can stop trying.

STANDING ALONE IN INTEGRITY

There is something that can be found in one place. It is a great treasure, which may be called the fulfillment of existence. The place where this treasure can be found is the place on which one stands.

—Martin Buber

There is nothing to escape from — and nothing to escape to. One is always alone.

—T. S. Eliot

We don't get much support for our inquiry into actuality. The social structures in which we exist probably won't help us. Our relatives and friends will generally be aghast. Even our own minds will rebel.

Consider this a warning. All those who are inquiring stand alone in the universe. There is no reliable support, there is only our integrity as a guide. Even relationships forged in the understanding of this exploration, by their nature, must challenge, not coddle us.

Deep questioning of our existence is not for the fainthearted or the dilettante. Such exploration will disrupt, transform, and change the entirety of our perspective, because the perspective comes from a "me" that isn't there. This thin veil of illusion, once pierced, will always be pierced.

It is important that we bring tremendous order to our life, that there is a solid foundation created in the very reality that we are exploring. It is easy to say that reality is just thought. It is very challenging to live that perception in a world that is impregnated with thought of all kinds.

Order comes through fearlessly addressing issues of money, work, relationship, family, and responsibility, not running from them. Too many of us hide from our life in the name of spirituality. Too many of us say life is an illusion, when in actuality, we are the illusion. The illusion lies in how we cling to our conditioning, our ideas, our self.

Standing alone in the actuality of life means taking full responsibility for the entirety of our life. We won't be acknowledged for that. We won't be considered spiritual. Without the solid foundation, without order in our life, we cannot perceive anything but the mess we have created through avoidance. But, in dealing with our life fully, we can be free of the entanglements of a disorderly existence and have the basis for a further inquiry.

No one can give us directions on how to live with integrity. No one can certify that we are living our perceptions.

We stand alone, where we are. This is the portal to the whole of life.

CRISIS AND CHANGE — WE ARE THE WHIRLED

The world is in crisis. Our rain forests are being logged and burned. Our oceans and waterways are becoming increasingly polluted. The greenhouse effect is melting the polar ice caps. The world is overpopulating at an alarming rate. Crime is up. Crazies shoot and bomb randomly. Global terrorism threatens us with everything from stolen nuclear warheads to horrific bioweaponry.

We contemplate this morass and our minds whirl with the vast complexity of it all. We have no idea what to do about any of it. Yet it is critical to change it, before it is too late.

We try to think globally and act locally. We recycle our plastic, glass, and paper. We send a check to the Sierra Club. We try to ride our bicycles more. We have a sinking feeling that we aren't really making a difference in anything, and we're probably right.

We try engaged spirituality. We strive to put together an understanding of the inner with the problems of the outer. Our minds still whirl, but now we can find a focus from which to act. We march, we organize, we write letters and raise money. We are at least engaged with the world's problems. But we also know that these problems seem to be unmoved by our involvement. We still aren't making a difference.

Our minds still whirl. Our minds have never stopped whirling. No matter how much we have done about the problems we see around us, the problems keep on.

This is for a simple reason.

We are the whirled.

The problem isn't just in the world, it is in us as the whirled, and as the world.

There is no inner and outer. There is no engaged spirituality. The whirled is the world. There is nothing to engage that is outside the movement of our own conceptualization. And there is no place to stand from which to engage this constant flow of interpretation.

Thought has divided the world. Conveniently the problem is out there, or in there, but not here, now.

Thought has got it wrong. There is only one crisis, and it is a total crisis. The crisis is thought itself, our belief in it, our identification with it and with its bastard child, the "me."

We divert our attention from the actuality of our conflicted mind structures and try to believe that we will bring about a world free from conflict. But that which is in conflict is not going to create the end of conflict.

The "me" is conflict itself, it has no intention or means to bring conflict to an end.

Thought creates an inner world and an outer world. These are concepts, not actual.

If the inner and outer are the same, and if we see the crisis all around us, then we are also seeing the crisis that is us.

Let us engage the crisis that is us not from a spiritual perspective but from the direct contact with who and what we are. If this is a crisis, there is no delay, no retreat, no time.

Are we ready now for radical change, revolutionary change, total change? Has the total crisis that we have discovered brought us to a point where the resistance to change ceases?

The whirled stops.

The world stops.

Thought stops.

The "me" stops.

In one moment, action, change, healing express spontaneously from this silence.

IMPERMANENCE, PAIN,
EMPTINESS, AND COMPASSION

Twenty-five hundred years ago the Buddha suggested that life was impermanent, uncomfortable, and inherently empty. From everything we can see in our postmodern paved paradise, it appears he got it right on the money.

A few short centuries later, Jesus came along and, without getting too involved in the existential dilemma, directed us, specifically and unequivocally, to love each other. From everything we can find out through direct investigation, that love, the compassion of our mutuality, is the only real chance we have for realizing an integrated life.

The Buddha suggests that we consider impermanence, pain, emptiness, and Jesus adds compassion.

Our thoughts, feelings, and sense impressions seem to arise and fall away without any permanent qualities remaining. We seem to find attractions and dislikes in almost everything, leaving ourselves in a state of dissatisfaction, a kind of dull, simmering pain. We can't find a self, a center, a "me," no matter how hard we try. We seem to be made up of, well, nothing.

When we look at this combination of aspects of our existence pointed out so clearly by the Buddha, we might also notice that we avoid acknowledging that this is our nature. We like to act, to believe, to pretend that it just isn't so. We like to pretend that we are each a "me" that is rock solid, ongoing, and quite comfortable, thank you.

We are terrified by the understanding that we are actually the universe. We are the power, the glory, the wisdom, the everything. We are not really just the owner of the mint-condition 1968 Ford Fairlane, or the holder of the certificate of deposit down at the bank where we locked in the rate just before interest rates dropped, or the parent of the junior soccer league star halfback. We are not the aspect of the whole; we are actually the whole.

Buddha was not just suggesting that we are nothing, he was pointing out that because we are nothing, we are everything. That's a lot. Buddhists have been thinking about that for the last few millennia.

Jesus put the icing on the cake by directing us to love our neighbor as ourselves, which is about all we have left to do when we are everything.

These are straightforward operating instructions. You are everything, so love your neighbor, who, by the way, happens to be yourself, anyway.

But it is far too simple to think of it that way, so we had to create thousands of books to explain what these visionaries were saying. Now there are various schools of thought, churches, sects, priests, teachers, and systems we can choose from. It is truly confusing, and we are relieved to be confused. Otherwise we would have had to live the simplicity of love.

We're afraid to step out of our fear, and to love. We're all alike. And it's a good thing, too.

In the recognition that the human condition is all of us, that we're all alike, we find that compassion arises.

We know why people do the destructive and devious things they do, because we know why we do them.

We are them. We are the human condition. And, knowing this, unavoidably we find compassion, connection, we fall in love.

We fall in love with ourselves, with each other, with the human condition.

Love, in the end, doesn't come from being loving. It comes from being human. It comes from our failure to love and from our fear of love. The mythic Jesus, after all, was incarnate as a human being. He had all the passions of a human and all the failures. In between some fairly impressive miracles, he perceived that the other is ourself.

That's the miracle.

The other is ourself, because, in fact, there is no self to be other, and no other to be other.

Jesus and Buddha were saying the same thing. How could they not? There was no Buddha. There was no Jesus.

There is only impermanence, dissatisfaction, emptiness, and love. And there is none of that.

There is nothing.

And there is not that, either.

EXPRESSING THE UNIVERSAL IN WHAT IS

To arrive where you are, to get from where you are not,
You must go by a way wherein there is no ecstasy.
In order to arrive at what you do not know
You must go by the way which is the way of ignorance.

— T.S. Eliot

You Can't Get There from Here or Anywhere Else, Either

Apart from the known and the unknown, what else
is there?

— Harold Pinter

A man was traveling to visit his relatives in another state.
He decided to take a scenic back way, and after driving
most of the day, realized he was totally lost. The man
spotted a farmer standing by his field and stopped to ask
him directions to the city where his kin lived.

The farmer thought about it for a while, and then
said, "Well, sir, you head up this road about five miles and
turn left . . . no, that's not it.Okay, go down that road
about ten miles to the fork . . . no, that's not it. . . ."

The farmer stopped and, after considering the prob-
lem very thoroughly, said, "I am sorry, but you can't get
there from here."

For millennia humankind has relied on religious structures to interpret and explain the mysteries of life and death. For as many

years, spiritual teachings have been passed down through hierarchical structures. These were sometimes patriarchal, sometimes matriarchal, but always authority based. Very few voices in all this time have suggested that truth did not emanate from a center but from the whole. These few voices were anomalies, curiosities, obscurities. They were ignored.

But now the structures of spiritual power are shifting. The struggle in today's spiritual world occurs between religious fundamentalism and moral relativism, between the certain knowledge of belief and the moral chaos of believing in nothing. Certainty is crumbling. Belief is crumbling. Chaos is taking over.

Mystical revelation may be the expression of truth, but the religious institutions that grow out of authentic insights are built on ignorance, designed by bureaucrats, and maintained through power, fear, and threat. A global culture is no longer so easy to convince of theological certainties. The global village can be sold Coke and Nike, but absolute truth is a bit trickier. It is too easy to switch channels to some other absolute truth. Or the made-for-TV version of absolute truth. When there are multiple absolute truths, there are no absolute truths. Just as orthodox believers of every religion have always warned, ecumenicalism is the doom of religious certainty.

Moral relativism leaves us in a quandary. If everything is a social construction, including religious verities, then nothing is right or wrong, right?

Now Moses delivers the "Ten Suggestions," and the Noble Eightfold Path is rewritten as "Eight Steps to a New You" and featured in pop New Age media outlets. Kids learn how to clarify their values in school based on experiencing many viewpoints and deciding for themselves what is right and wrong. Progressive parents choose from endless recombinations of Orthodox, Conservative, or Reform Judeo-Christian-Sufi-Buddhist-Channeled-Energy-Work-Nondenominational-Once-a-Week-with-Childcare-Provided Relative Truth (Version 7.0 for Windows).

Justice is meted out live on CNN and Court TV and through the wisdom of the Shiva/Shakti of American Jurisprudence, Judges Judy and Wapner.

The democratic ideal has degenerated into governing through the dervishes of spin control, media leaks, overnight polls, and sound bites.

Community takes place through untold millions of miles of wires on the World Wide Web and cable television, where we can count Ally and Dharma among our Friends and where we live next to the Simpsons in South Park as we gleefully chant, "Oh, no, they killed Kenny!" We experience our greatest aspirations with the cyborgs and empaths in future deep-space treks and steroid-soaked gladiators bashing each other on Super Sunday. We experience our deepest fears flipping through the files marked X. Virtual reality isn't the future, it is virtually here.

We don't believe in any absolute truth. We can't believe in moral relativism and the culture of compromise. And to make matters worse, apparently God is dead.

Don't Believe Anything

What if God was one of us? / just a slob like one of us?

—Joan Osborne

God isn't dead, belief is. The postmodern world we inhabit has deconstructed belief so thoroughly that all that is left to believe is that there is nothing to believe.

This last remaining belief is that there are no absolutes. Morality is relative. Belief is a social construction. Reality is a function of our culture, education, language.

We used to believe in America, democracy, Mom, apple pie, God. But then drugs, rock and roll, Vietnam, and the counterculture destroyed most of the absolutes that we had all agreed were solid realities. The Counterculture Sell-Out Because We're Older Now and Have to Pay the Mortgage deconstructed the deconstruction, leaving generation X an inheritance of ever-deepening cynicism.

This new generation tried expressing itself with slacking, depression, grunge, body piercing, and launching flimflam sci-fi high-tech Wall Street IPOs with names like Netscape and Yahoo that suck up their ex-hippie parents' 401-Ks. The boomers have social security paid for by the Xers, the Xers have stock options paid for by boomers' retirement funds, and those who are retired now are just happy that they are going to die before the whole thing collapses.

The generation that is just now coming to adulthood, generation.com, looks at all that has come before them with growing alarm. Where is the delete button?

Nobody believes in anything anymore—except certain funda-mentalists, who believe very hard in certain things, even though fundamentalists are always disagreeing with each other over their beliefs. (When you have absolute beliefs, those arguments go on for a long time and occupy most of your energy, so you hardly have time to plan your attacks on people who don't believe in anything and who should probably be considered the real bar-barians).

But for those who don't believe in belief, nonbelief is a stance that is very enlightened, very modern—and very suspect. We have constructed this nonbelief through the mechanisms of our culture, our philosophy, and our education, all of which are belief systems in themselves. We have, in fact, simply constructed a new belief.

What happens when we puncture this last belief? Does God finally speak? Would God speak after all these millennia of si-lence?

Thousands of years have passed while people worshiped graven images, followed others' interpretations of the divine, and settled for liturgy, theology, and ritual in the place of mystic com-munion. All of the prophets have long ago been replaced by priests.

But suddenly, in a spasm of cultural realization, the God of Belief is declared dead, and then Belief is declared dead and cyn-icism is crowned the last word on the subject. This is workable. God is held in abeyance and there is no punishment for our wicked ways, because who believes in wicked ways, let alone punishment?

Things are going along fine. Interest rates are low. The mar-

ket is breaking new highs. Then something happens. Maybe this
is God getting impatient and tickling us a bit, but we notice that
cynicism is a belief, too. Not only that, but it's not very enjoyable.

In the last part of the twentieth century of the Christian era as
we move into the third millennium, what if we declared the end
of *all* beliefs? What if, in that realization, cynicism, which is, after
all, a belief, vaporized? What if we deconstructed deconstruction?

Would God finally speak? Would we be left with the direct
contact with the divine, which is all that is left when everything
else has been stripped away? Would we have finally passed
through the collective Dark Night of the Soul, the cultural Kali
Yuga that we have been stuck in? Would we want to hear what
God had to say? What would we say to God? Could we look directly at the face of God?

No, this couldn't happen. God is dead.

But is it so? Is God dead? Or is it belief that is dead? (Perhaps
it is like the famous graffiti: God isn't dead, but alive and working on a much less ambitious project.)

Listen very carefully. Look around. What is expressed when
belief is silent?

Is God speaking to us? Do we want to hear what God has to
say?

Don't believe in God, don't believe in the self, and certainly
don't believe anything that is written here.

What if God spoke to us and commanded us not to believe in
God? What if, in that moment, as all belief collapsed, God and
the self collapsed with it?

Now what is there?

ACTUALITY — WE ARE ALREADY HERE

Listen: there's a hell
Of a good universe next door; let's go
—E. E. Cummings, *1X1*

We have believed in belief for so long that we have not considered the possibility that belief simply isn't necessary, nor does its absence dictate chaos. We don't need to believe in a truth, nor do we need to believe in multiple truths or even no truth. We don't need to believe in belief.

We have available to us the material of existence, the actuality of our life. The actuality of life includes belief but is not defined by it. This is because the actuality of belief is that it is conceptual, thought, idea, conditioning. We do not live without belief in actuality, but we live free of its limitation.

Actuality is not a choice. It is the fact.

Actuality is not a belief. It occurs without our ideation, without our involvement, without our interpretation.

Actuality also occurs with our ideation, our involvement, and our interpretation.

Actuality includes everything, and everything is really big. It's bigger than me, bigger than you, and bigger than us. It is bigger than all the ideas, beliefs, religions, and philosophies put together, because it includes all of these . . . and more. Actuality includes everything we can collect, describe, remember, imagine, and project, plus everything else.

We can't have actuality, we can't get actuality, we can't become actuality. Actuality is here. We are already here.

We can describe here. That's actuality.

We can be unaware of here. That's actuality.

We can be angry here. That's actuality.

We can be confused and neurotic and wish we were here, which we are convinced we are not. That's actuality.

This vast all and everything is actuality. We are that vastness. We are all and everything. We are actuality. We are already here.

Getting to Where You Are and Staying There

One thing, all things:
move among and intermingle,
without distinction.
To live in this realization
is to be without anxiety about nonperfection.

—Sengstan, Third Zen Patriarch

We are where we are. We're the vastness. We're all and everything. Now how do we stay there?

We've had the experience so many times of getting to that high, that flow, that place of nonseparation, only to come crashing back into our "me." How do we stay there?

The answer is simple.

There is here.

Staying there is easy.

There is here.

There aren't two places to be. There isn't a choice. There isn't a good and a bad place. There aren't two places. There is one place. Here, there, everywhere is one. We are always in one place. Staying there is the fact.

States of mind come and go. Thoughts and feelings arise and pass away. We're not going anywhere, thought is going somewhere. We don't have anywhere to go that isn't where we already are.

What we are is a vantage point, a perspective, an aspect of thought itself. Thought, by its nature, creates the sense of duality, of subject/object. When it arises, we arise as the subject part of the thought.

That's where we are.

Thought decays into nothingness. Another thought arises. We arise as the subject part of the thought.

That's where we are.

And so on and on.

We say we should be aware of this process, and not just live unconsciously. When this thought arises, we arise as the subject part of the thought.

That's where we are.

We pay attention and notice the nature of thought, how it arises and creates a subject, a "me." When this thought arises, we arise as the subject part of the thought.

That's where we are.

When thought of any kind occurs, we occur as the subject. When feelings occur, we occur. When any knowing occurs, we occur.

We are always where we are.

We're not going anywhere, because we can't get anywhere.

Now when the thoughts fall silent, in the space between thoughts, where are we?

AFTERWORD

ACTUALITY, LOVE, AND HAPPINESS

*If rationality were the criterion for things being allowed
to exist, the world would be one gigantic field of
soya beans.*

—Tom Stoppard

Let us not misconstrue the deconstruction of meditation, our relationships, our life, our activities to mean the end of them. We
live in a relative world in which we must embrace the life that we
are living in full. Understanding the relative nature, the conceptual nature, of our life allows that full embrace.

We may understand that we are not the conceptual frame-
works in which we live and relate, but this is the medium in
which we must function.

If we are to love, let us love fully. Let us love in the absolute
world of silence. And let us love in the relative world of our husband or wife, our children, our friends and neighbors. These two
worlds, in the end, are one world.

If we can find the boundarylessness of our actual nature, we
can also bring that quality into the world of limitation and form.

Our inquiry is not intended to bring about some understanding that excludes us from participating in the life around us.
Rather, it is to bring that insight with us into the workplace, the
school, the home, and the community.

This integral understanding demands tremendous concern for the details of our life. When we bring this quality into our day-to-day life, our life is changed, and our changed life changes us.

This is the crucible of life's alchemy, the meeting place of inner and outer, of form and formless. Here we discover the explosion of exuberance, of feeling, which is a life lived.

Living is what we are doing with or without our philosophies, our meditation techniques, our religions. Living is the expression of relatedness of all of life. We need not fear it. We need not control it. We need not contain it. We can simply live.

We can relax. The universal is expressing itself right now, without our effort. The pressure to perform is off. We don't have to sit cross-legged in pain. We don't have to read esoteric tomes explaining the mysteries of the universe.

Without the mind's interpretation, the universe is whole and undivided.

And even with the mind's activity, the universe is whole and undivided. Our minds just happen to be cluttered with phone numbers and addresses, facts and figures, likes and dislikes.

The universe is a cluttered universe. It is a cluttered, whole, and undivided universe.

The mind cannot resolve this paradox.

We can relax.

The whole does not require us to figure it out, only that we live in the fullness of life. Our inquiry is not just the search for an explanation but the discovery of life itself in the actuality of each moment.

ABOUT THE AUTHOR

Steven Harrison is the author of *The Question to Life's Answers, Being One, Doing Nothing,* and *The Happy Child.* He is a founder of All Together Now International, a charitable organization that aids street children and the destitute in South Asia. He is also a founder of The Living School, a learning community in Boulder, Colorado, where he lives.

Those interested may write:

    Steven Harrison
    P O Box 6071
    Boulder, CO 80306
    InDialog@aol.com
    www.doingnothing.com

For more information:

    The Living School
    P O Box 6105
    Boulder, CO 80306
    Email: contact@LivingSchool.org
    www.LivingSchool.org

    All Together Now International
    P O Box 7111
    Boulder, CO 80306
    AllToNow@aol.com
    www.alltogether.org

Sentient Publications, LLC publishes books on cultural creativity, experimental education, transformative spirituality, holistic health, new science, ecology, and other topics, approached from an integral viewpoint. Our authors are intensely interested in exploring the nature of life from fresh perspectives, addressing life's great questions, and fostering the full expression of the human potential. Sentient Publications' books arise from the spirit of inquiry and the richness of the inherent dialogue between writer and reader.

Our Culture Tools series is designed to give social catalyzers and cultural entrepreneurs the essential information, technology, and inspiration to forge a sustainable, creative, and compassionate world.

We are very interested in hearing from our readers. To direct suggestions or comments to us, or to be added to our mailing list, please contact:

SENTIENT PUBLICATIONS, LLC
1113 Spruce Street
Boulder, CO 80302
303-443-2188
contact@sentientpublications.com
www.sentientpublications.com